The Ancient Worlds Atlas

Written by Dr. Anne Millard

Illustrated by Russell Barnett

DK

DK Penguin Random House

REVISED EDITION

DK LONDON   **DK INDIA**

Senior Editor   **Desk Editor**
Fleur Star   Saumya Agarwal
Project Art Editor   **Managing Editor**
Gregory McCarthy   Saloni Singh
Senior Art Editor   **Senior Art Editor**
Jane Ewart   Vikas Chauhan
Managing Editor   **Managing Art Editor**
Lindsay Kent   Govind Mittal
Managing Art Editor   **Senior Picture Researcher**
Michelle Baxter   Sumedha Chopra
Production Editor   **DTP Designers**
Jacqueline Street-Elkayam   Rajdeep Singh, Syed Md Farhan
Senior Production Controller   Umesh Singh Rawat, Rakesh Kumar
Rachel Ng   **Jacket Designer**
Jacket Design Development Manager   Vidushi Chaudhry
Sophia MTT   **Senior Jackets Coordinator**
Publisher   Priyanka Sharma Saddi
Andrew Macintyre
Art Director
Karen Self
Publishing Director
Jonathan Metcalf

Consultant
Philip Parker

FIRST EDITION
Art Editor Lester Cheeseman
Project Editor Fran Jones
Production Shelagh Gibson
Managing Editor Susan Peach
Managing Art Editor Jacquie Gulliver

History consultants
Dr. David Anderson, History Department, School of Oriental
and African Studies, University of London
Penny Bateman, Education Service, British Museum, London
Lucy Anne Bishop, The Horniman Museum, London
George Hart, Education Service, British Museum, London
Stephanie Haygarth, Australian Institute of Aboriginal and
Torres Strait Islander Studies, Canberra
Dr. Simon James, Education Service, British Museum, London
Professor Robert Layton, Department of Anthropology,
University of Durham
Dr. John Marr, Bhavan Institute of Indian Culture, London
Dr. Keith Nicklin, The Horniman Museum, London
Carl Phillips, Institute of Archaeology, London
Jane Portal, Department of Oriental Antiquities,
British Museum, London
Jill Varndell, Education Service, British Museum, London

This American Edition, 2023
First American Edition, 1994
Published in the United States by DK Publishing
1745 Broadway, 20th Floor, New York, NY 10019
Copyright © 1994, 2023 Dorling Kindersley Limited
DK, a Division of Penguin Random House LLC
23 24 25 26 27 10 9 8 7 6 5 4 3 2 1
001–334263–Apr/2023

A catalog record for this book is available from the Library of Congress.
ISBN 978-0-7440-7726-1

Printed and bound in Malaysia

For the curious
www.dk.com

MIX
Paper | Supporting
responsible forestry
FSC™ C018179

This book was made with Forest
Stewardship Council™ certified
paper – one small step in DK's
commitment to a sustainable future.
For more information go to
www.dk.com/our-green-pledge

CONTENTS

Mapping the Past

THIS ATLAS TELLS THE STORY of how people lived in the ancient world. It also shows where the world's greatest civilizations were located and how they developed in very different environments. The book starts in the Middle East in the hot, crowded cities of Sumer in 4000 BCE and finishes high in the Andes Mountains of South America with the Incas in 1500 CE. Each of the peoples included in the book have left their mark on history, often for very different reasons. The Egyptians, for example, built huge pyramid tombs, the Chinese developed some remarkable inventions, the Romans organized vast armies, and the Greeks introduced theatre and the Olympic Games.

Civilizations and cultures

This book covers many different peoples—most of them described as civilizations. The word "civilization" is used for a group of people who have reached an advanced stage of development. This usually means they have organized methods of farming and a large population settled in towns and cities. They have developed a system of writing, worked out a method of government, and built monuments for their gods and rulers. But the word civilization is sometimes extended to cover other peoples, too. These may be groups who did not write, such as the Celts, or peoples who, like the First Australians, chose not to live in cities, but still created a rich and unique culture of their own.

Many early civilizations worshipped gods and goddesses. The Egyptians built decorated temples for their gods, some of whom are shown here.

Once people did not have to spend all their time growing food, they developed new skills. This craftworker is decorating a wooden coffin.

Writing was one feature of a civilization. The Egyptians used hieroglyphs to keep records.

The first great civilizations grew in fertile river valleys. Water from the Nile River was guided into fields. Enough crops were grown to feed the growing populations.

Domesticated animals made tasks easier. Cattle pulled plows to prepare the ground for sowing.

This Egyptian tomb wall painting shows some of the ways in which organized farming created the wealth necessary for a civilization to develop. The tomb was built in about 1290 BCE for Sennedjem, one of the workers who decorated the pharaohs' tombs.

Mud was shaped into bricks to build homes in the world's first cities.

The invention of tools helped farmers. Here, sickles with flint blades are used to cut corn.

As society developed, some people grew wealthy. They could afford fine linen clothes made from these flax plants.

Egyptian agriculture was so successful that farmers were able to grow a wide range of food, including date palms.

Dating systems

In this book you will find references to the Stone Age, the Bronze Age, and the Iron Age. These are based on the tools and weapons most used by a particular civilization and cannot be used to identify specific dates worldwide because they happened at different times. The Bronze Age in the Middle East, for example, began hundreds of years earlier than in China. Elsewhere in the text, dates after the names of rulers such as King Darius (522–486 BCE) give the time of their reign. Dates are also divided into BCE (Before Common Era) or CE (Common Era). An approximate date is shown as c.1200 BCE (c. stands for *circa*, or about).

The Great Wall of China was built to protect the Chinese from northern invaders. Features such as mountain ranges or rivers also created natural barriers.

The changing world

Many of the landscapes shown in this book do not look the same today. Over thousands of years, rivers alter their courses, new islands are born when a volcano erupts under the sea, and coastlines change. People affect the landscape, too. At one time, Europe was covered in thick forests, long since chopped down for fuel and building materials. The northern edge of the Sahara Desert was once fertile enough to provide crops for Rome. In addition, borders between territories changed many times.

How to use the atlas

Each of the maps in this book looks at a different civilization. The one below shows the Roman Empire. Each map features major towns, cities, and trade routes that were important at the time. Small scenes of daily life are located as closely as possible to where they happened. The maps also show the physical features, such as deserts, mountains, and lakes, that affected how people lived.

Surrounding areas
Areas in the pale yellow color were not part of the civilization featured on those pages. They are included to show the lands, and possible enemies, that lay beyond the territory of the people.

Special features
Many pages in the atlas have special illustrated scenes that explain part of the story on that page. This view shows the layout of a Roman army fort. Other views might show inside a house, or the layout of a city.

Where in the world
Every map has a globe. The red area on the globe shows the location of the civilization featured on that map.

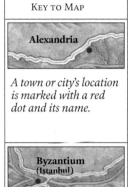

Key to Map

Alexandria

A town or city's location is marked with a red dot and its name.

Byzantium (Istanbul)

If a town has a different modern name, it may be shown in parentheses underneath.

Italica

Symbols, such as this amphitheatre, show the location of ancient sites or buildings.

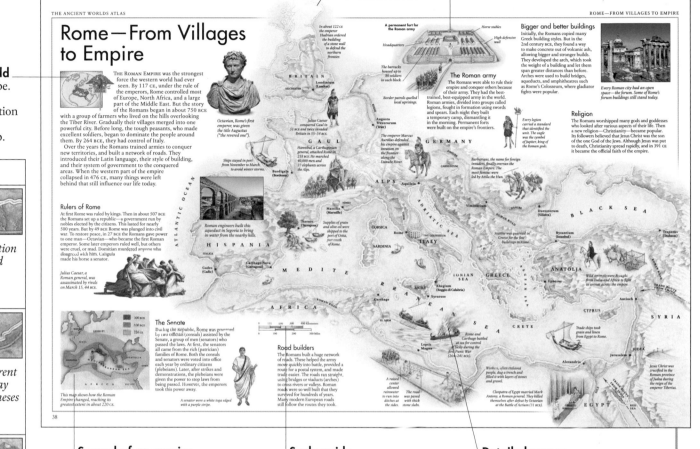

Spread of an empire
On some pages, small inset maps show how an empire expanded beyond the area of the main map. Areas are shown in different colors with dates that explain when that part of the empire was conquered.

Scale guide
Use this scale to figure out the size of the area shown on the map. You can also calculate the length of an ancient road or the distance from one city to another. Not all the maps are drawn to the same scale.

Detailed scenes
Illustrated scenes show how people passed their time— fighting, playing, working, or worshipping their gods. Each scene, such as this sea battle, is located as closely as possible to the place where it happened.

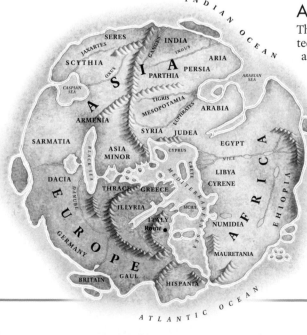

An ancient view of the world

The maps in this book are based on modern mapping techniques. But before the world was mapped out as it is today, people only understood the extent of the world as they knew it. Map makers, known as cartographers, based maps on their own experience, and unknown territory was often shown full of terrifying creatures. They put the direction they thought was most important at the top. Many people's ideas of the world were based on religious beliefs about how their gods created the world. The ancient Indians, for example, believed the world was held on a turtle's back.

This illustration is based on a Roman world map from the 1st century BCE. It shows how mapmakers thought the Roman Empire took up most of the world.

The Arab map maker al-Idrisi created this map of the world in 1154 CE. Unlike the Romans, the Arabs put south at the top.

Where People Lived

MANY THOUSANDS OF YEARS AGO, people wandered the world in search of food, finding shelter in caves or in tents made of animal skins. They hunted animals and gathered fruits, nuts, and whatever vegetables they could find. But in about 10,000 BCE, the first farming began within an arc of land known as the Fertile Crescent in the Middle East. Gradually, farming spread throughout Europe. It also developed independently in other areas of the world, including the Americas, Africa, and Asia. Farming enabled people to control their food supply. For the first time, they could stay in one place all year round, and villages and towns began to develop.

By about 4000 BCE, the time when this book starts, people had begun to settle, and soon the first great civilization—Sumer—had sprung up between the Tigris and Euphrates rivers in modern-day Iraq. Over the next 5,000 years, the period of time covered by this book, the civilizations shown on these maps developed around the world.

Inuit
c.1000 CE onwards

YUKON

Makah
c.1300–1500 CE

NORTH AMERICA

MISSOURI

Indigenous people of the Plains
c.250 BCE onward

Pueblo people
c.750 CE onwards

Hopewell
c.200–550 CE

Adena
c.1000 BCE–200 CE

MISSISSIPPI

Mississippians
c.700–1500 CE

Olmecs
c.1200–400 BCE

Aztecs
c.1200–1519 CE

Maya
c.250–900 CE

Celts
c.750 BCE–100 CE

Monument Builders
c.2500–1000 BCE

A T L A N T I C

Ghanaians
c.700–1200 CE

O C E A N

AMAZON

Inca
c.1200–1532 CE

SOUTH AMERICA

P A C I F I C

O C E A N

Polynesians
c.2000 BCE onwards

This scene from Iraq shows the fertile land and mud-brick houses along the Tigris River.

River valleys

It is no coincidence that the first great civilizations—Sumer, Egypt, China, and the Indus Valley—all grew beside large rivers. There were enormous advantages. As well as offering a constant supply of fresh water for crops, the rivers provided a method of transporting heavy materials for building, and a route for boats to bring goods from abroad. People prospered and populations grew. Farmers produced so much food that people were free to develop specialized skills—they became potters, weavers, metalworkers, and builders.

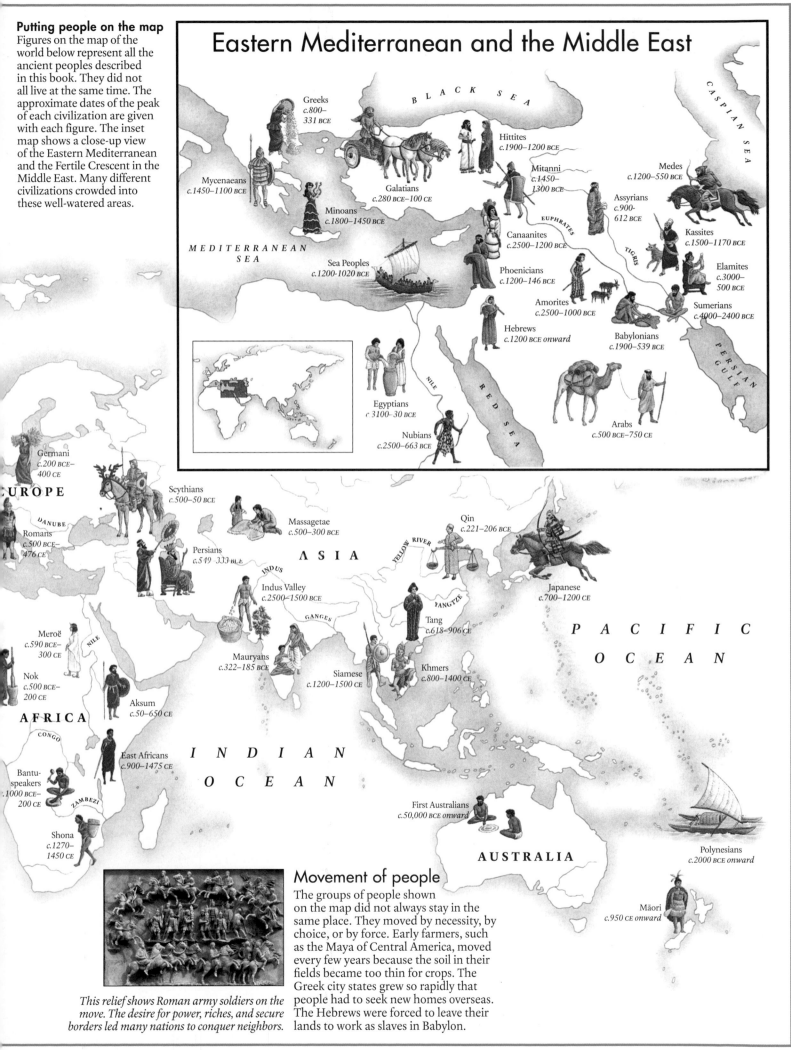

Putting people on the map
Figures on the map of the world below represent all the ancient peoples described in this book. They did not all live at the same time. The approximate dates of the peak of each civilization are given with each figure. The inset map shows a close-up view of the Eastern Mediterranean and the Fertile Crescent in the Middle East. Many different civilizations crowded into these well-watered areas.

Eastern Mediterranean and the Middle East

BLACK SEA

Greeks
c.800–331 BCE

Hittites
c.1900–1200 BCE

Mitanni
c.1450–1300 BCE

Medes
c.1200–550 BCE

Galatians
c.280 BCE–100 CE

Assyrians
c.900–612 BCE

Mycenaeans
c.1450–1100 BCE

Kassites
c.1500–1170 BCE

Minoans
c.1800–1450 BCE

Canaanites
c.2500–1200 BCE

EUPHRATES

MEDITERRANEAN SEA

Sea Peoples
c.1200–1020 BCE

Phoenicians
c.1200–146 BCE

TIGRIS

Elamites
c.3000–500 BCE

Amorites
c.2500–1000 BCE

Sumerians
c.4000–2400 BCE

Hebrews
c.1200 BCE onward

Babylonians
c.1900–539 BCE

CASPIAN SEA

PERSIAN GULF

Egyptians
c.3100–30 BCE

NILE

RED SEA

Arabs
c.500 BCE–750 CE

Nubians
c.2500–663 BCE

Germani
c.200 BCE–400 CE

EUROPE

Scythians
c.500–50 BCE

Massagetae
c.500–300 BCE

Qin
c.221–206 BCE

DANUBE

Romans
c.500 BCE–476 CE

Persians
c.549–333 BCE

ASIA

YELLOW RIVER

INDUS

Japanese
c.700–1200 CE

Indus Valley
c.2500–1500 BCE

PACIFIC OCEAN

Meroë
c.590 BCE–300 CE

NILE

GANGES

YANGTZE

Tang
c.618–906 CE

Nok
c.500 BCE–200 CE

Mauryans
c.322–185 BCE

Siamese
c.1200–1500 CE

Khmers
c.800–1400 CE

Aksum
c.50–650 CE

AFRICA

CONGO

East Africans
c.900–1475 CE

INDIAN OCEAN

Bantu-speakers
c.1000 BCE–200 CE

ZAMBEZI

Shona
c.1270–1450 CE

First Australians
c.50,000 BCE onward

Polynesians
c.2000 BCE onward

AUSTRALIA

Māori
c.950 CE onward

Movement of people

The groups of people shown on the map did not always stay in the same place. They moved by necessity, by choice, or by force. Early farmers, such as the Maya of Central America, moved every few years because the soil in their fields became too thin for crops. The Greek city states grew so rapidly that people had to seek new homes overseas. The Hebrews were forced to leave their lands to work as slaves in Babylon.

This relief shows Roman army soldiers on the move. The desire for power, riches, and secure borders led many nations to conquer neighbors.

Clues to the Past

THIS BOOK IS FULL OF AMAZING DETAILS about people who lived thousands of years ago. But how do historians piece the information together and find out what buildings were like, what clothes people wore, where they traded, and what they grew for food?

The experts who study the lives of ancient people from the remains of what they built or made are called archaeologists. Material remains and written records form the basis for most of our knowledge about the past.

Sometimes these experts are lucky enough to find the remains of ancient buildings still standing—such as the Colosseum in Rome. More often, they have to dig to find walls and objects buried underground. Clues on the surface, such as coins or pieces of pottery, may suggest that an archaeological site is buried below. Other sites can be discovered by accident. For example, the life-size warriors of a terra-cotta army were found in China by workers who were digging a well.

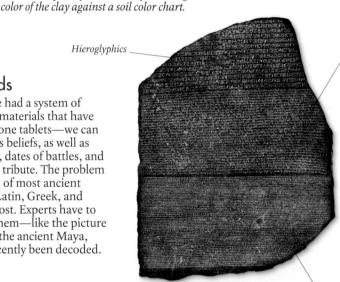

This map shows the location of Greek pottery finds. These can tell us about ancient trading networks as it is possible to tell where pottery was made by checking the color of the clay against a soil color chart.

Material evidence

Archaeologists learn about the past from objects people left behind. These may be the contents of graves, such as the furniture and jewelry found in the royal tombs of Ur. Stone carvings from the palaces of Assyria and Persia reveal details of life at the royal courts. Coins are often inscribed with the names and dates of rulers, so can be used to date the sites where they are found. Even the contents of ancient rubbish pits provide valuable insights.

Paintings on pottery give clues about daily life. This Greek vase shows the olive harvest.

Written records

If an ancient people had a system of writing—and used materials that have survived, such as stone tablets—we can learn about people's beliefs, as well as the names of rulers, dates of battles, and lists of items paid as tribute. The problem is that the meaning of most ancient languages, except Latin, Greek, and Chinese, has been lost. Experts have to learn how to read them—like the picture signs, or glyphs, of the ancient Maya, which have only recently been decoded.

Hieroglyphics

Demotic writing

The Rosetta Stone, discovered in 1799, held the key to deciphering Egyptian hieroglyphics. The same inscription was written three times—in hieroglyphics and demotic (two ancient Egyptian scripts) and in Greek. In all three, the name of Ptolemy (see right) appears. Applying the Greek letters in Ptolemy's name to other signs was the first step in deciphering the hieroglyphics.

Ancient Greek

Hieroglyphics

Demotic writing

Ancient Greek

Reconstructing a wooden house

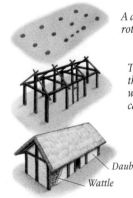

A dark patch, where wood has rotted, may indicate a post hole.

The hole's depth may suggest the size of the post, so the wall's height can be calculated.

Details can be filled in from other remains, such as the branches and mud (called wattle and daub) used for walls.

Daub

Wattle

Built to last

In the past, people built their houses and monuments from available materials, such as reeds and mud from the river, or timber from the forests. Most did not worry whether their homes would outlast them, but when they built for the gods they wanted a structure to last. So temples were built of stone or from bricks baked hard in the sun, and many of these buildings have survived. The homes of ordinary people have not, but experts can get an insight into what they were like from evidence left behind.

This Maya stone temple was discovered at Palenque, Mexico, in 1952. It survived being overgrown by the rainforest.

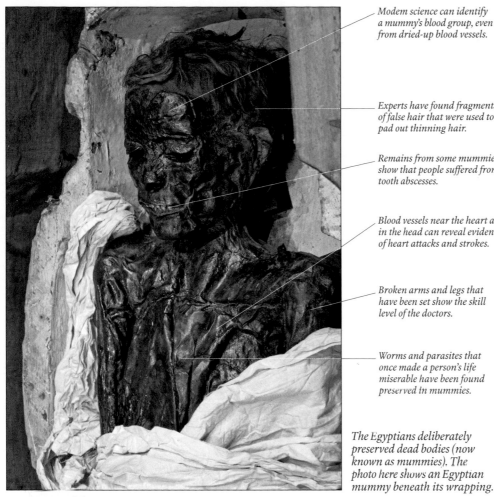

Modern science can identify a mummy's blood group, even from dried-up blood vessels.

Experts have found fragments of false hair that were used to pad out thinning hair.

Remains from some mummies show that people suffered from tooth abscesses.

Blood vessels near the heart and in the head can reveal evidence of heart attacks and strokes.

Broken arms and legs that have been set show the skill level of the doctors.

Worms and parasites that once made a person's life miserable have been found preserved in mummies.

The Egyptians deliberately preserved dead bodies (now known as mummies). The photo here shows an Egyptian mummy beneath its wrapping.

Face mapping

Thanks to mummification, we can look into the faces of ancient Egyptians. Specialists can also reconstruct a face from the remains of a skull, a process known as "face mapping." First a plaster cast is made of the skull. Then, based on the skull's shape, the face muscles are built up with modeling clay. A layer of material to represent flesh is added and features marked in. The pictures below show how experts reconstructed a 2,300-year-old skull, thought to be Princess Ada, a friend of Alexander the Great.

The process started with a skull, complete with its jaw and remaining teeth.

A plaster cast was made and pegs used as a guide to build up levels of muscle on the face.

Flesh was laid over the muscle. Ears, eyes, and nose were added to give a lifelike appearance.

Hair was added and the flesh was painted to give the face natural tones.

Preserved by nature

Certain natural elements preserve things for longer than usual. Egypt's dry heat has helped preserve bodies and objects placed in tombs. At the other extreme, the frozen body of a man who died almost 5,000 years ago was found in the Alps. In the right conditions, salt water can also preserve objects, for example, a Mycenaean ship and its contents, which sank off the Greek coast at Uluburan. In a more dramatic way, the eruption of Mount Vesuvius in 79 CE threw out hot ash that preserved many objects

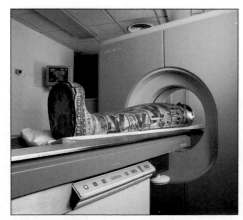

A mummy case enters a CT (computed tomography) scanner. This may reveal its sex, age, and cause of death.

Aerial photography can reveal signs of ancient sites beneath the ground. Crops grow taller and greener where the soil is deeper.

Modern dating techniques

Once items are discovered they need to be dated. If an ancient people could write, we can usually date events from their inscriptions. With other civilizations, experts can give approximate dates to the layers on an archaeological site by comparing finds with those from a culture that they can date. More precise dating is possible with modern techniques. Radiocarbon dating is used to date plant and animal remains. It measures the radioactivity being given off by carbon 14 atoms—the older an object, the less radioactivity. Thermoluminescence measures the light released from pottery objects. Some other dating techniques are shown here.

Dendrochronology is dating by counting tree rings. As trees grow, rings form in the trunk. In good years the rings are wide; in bad years, narrow. When experts find wood from various periods where some rings match, they count back from the present and date the piece accurately.

Sumer—The First Cities

MORE THAN 5,000 YEARS AGO the world's first cities were already bustling places. Situated around the Tigris and Euphrates rivers in what is now Iraq, cities such as Ur, Nippur, and Eridu had thousands of inhabitants. At the heart of each city, a temple tower, built to provide a home for the god, rose above the sprawl of mud-brick houses and workshops.

The area between the Tigris and Euphrates—later called Mesopotamia, meaning "land between two rivers"—was extremely fertile. It attracted the people we call Sumerians to settle there in about 5000 BCE. Although the weather was hot and dry, the rivers supplied the Sumerians with water to grow wheat, fruit, and vegetables. Their merchants traveled abroad, trading surplus food and items made by local artists. The population grew, and by about 3500 BCE, the original farming villages had expanded into a number of city states, each with its own ruler.

Sumerians invented the wheel, which they used in making pottery. Later a solid wooden wheel was developed to move the first wheeled carts and chariots.

Wandering tribes from the deserts were always trying to settle in the fertile lands. One group who succeeded were the Amorites.

The Big Man

A city's affairs were run by a Council of Elders. When war broke out they appointed a *lugal* (a "Big Man") to lead the army. As wars between the cities became more common, a *lugal* could hold on to power for longer, and sometimes for life. He also started to control daily life. Finally, he began appointing his sons to take over from him. The "Big Men" had become kings.

This peaceful scene from the Standard of Ur, a decorated wooden box found in a royal grave, shows rulers at a banquet. Farmers bring cattle and sheep as gifts.

Stairway to heaven

The Sumerians worshipped hundreds of gods and offerings were made every day to these gods, who people feared might otherwise punish them with unexpected floods, sickness, and wars. Each city also had a special god or goddess who was thought to own that city, and had a temple where people thought that god lived. The city of Ur was home to the moon god Nanna. Very early temples were rectangular buildings erected on low platforms. When a new temple was needed it was built on the ruins of the old one. This happened over and over again until temple platforms, called ziggurats, became huge, stepped structures with the temple on top.

The death pits of Ur

In the Sumerian city of Ur, archaeologists discovered the tombs of the early kings and queens. The remains showed what magnificent furniture, gold jewelry, musical instruments, and personal possessions the rulers owned. But that was not all. The tombs also contained the bodies of servants who had apparently agreed to commit suicide and be buried with their dead master or mistress so they could serve them in the next world.

This magnificent gold headdress was found on the body of a court lady in one of the royal graves of Ur.

Houses were built around open courtyards. There were no windows on the outside walls.

The ziggurat, or temple tower, at Ur was built by King Ur-Nammu in about 2100 BCE.

City of Ur

Tell Halaf

Mari

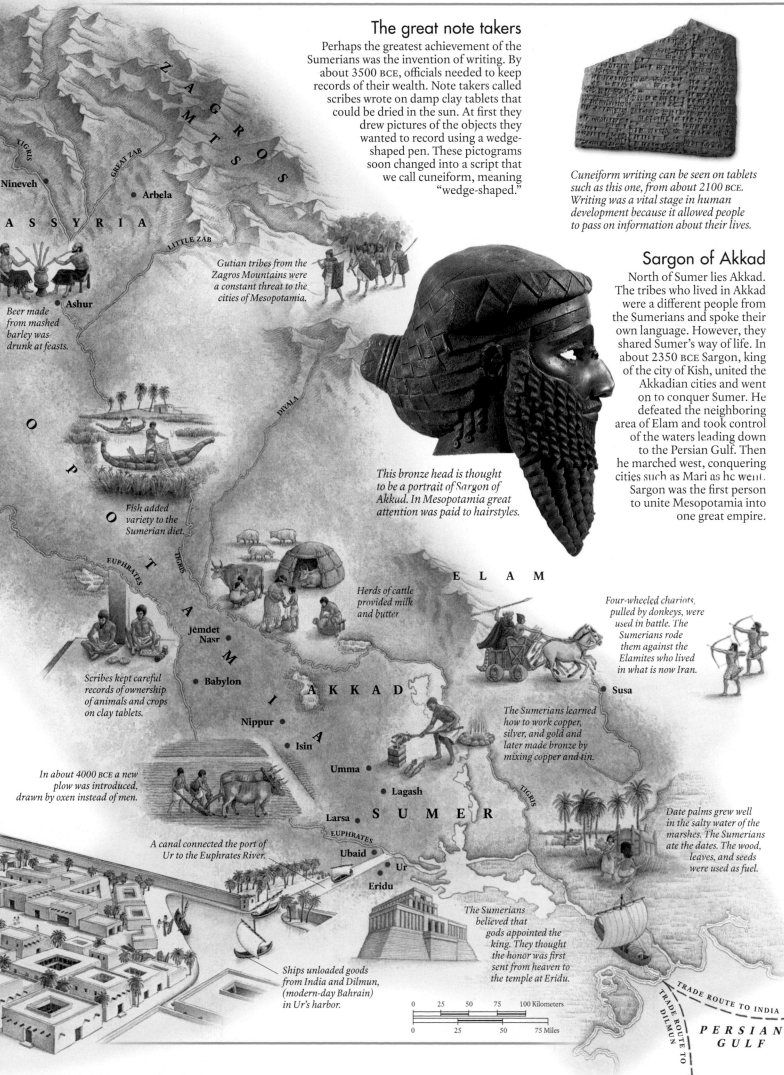

The great note takers

Perhaps the greatest achievement of the Sumerians was the invention of writing. By about 3500 BCE, officials needed to keep records of their wealth. Note takers called scribes wrote on damp clay tablets that could be dried in the sun. At first they drew pictures of the objects they wanted to record using a wedge-shaped pen. These pictograms soon changed into a script that we call cuneiform, meaning "wedge-shaped."

Cuneiform writing can be seen on tablets such as this one, from about 2100 BCE. Writing was a vital stage in human development because it allowed people to pass on information about their lives.

Sargon of Akkad

North of Sumer lies Akkad. The tribes who lived in Akkad were a different people from the Sumerians and spoke their own language. However, they shared Sumer's way of life. In about 2350 BCE Sargon, king of the city of Kish, united the Akkadian cities and went on to conquer Sumer. He defeated the neighboring area of Elam and took control of the waters leading down to the Persian Gulf. Then he marched west, conquering cities such as Mari as he went. Sargon was the first person to unite Mesopotamia into one great empire.

Gutian tribes from the Zagros Mountains were a constant threat to the cities of Mesopotamia.

Beer made from mashed barley was drunk at feasts.

This bronze head is thought to be a portrait of Sargon of Akkad. In Mesopotamia great attention was paid to hairstyles.

Fish added variety to the Sumerian diet.

Herds of cattle provided milk and butter

Four-wheeled chariots, pulled by donkeys, were used in battle. The Sumerians rode them against the Elamites who lived in what is now Iran.

Scribes kept careful records of ownership of animals and crops on clay tablets.

The Sumerians learned how to work copper, silver, and gold and later made bronze by mixing copper and tin.

In about 4000 BCE a new plow was introduced, drawn by oxen instead of men.

Date palms grew well in the salty water of the marshes. The Sumerians ate the dates. The wood, leaves, and seeds were used as fuel.

A canal connected the port of Ur to the Euphrates River.

The Sumerians believed that gods appointed the king. They thought the honor was first sent from heaven to the temple at Eridu.

Ships unloaded goods from India and Dilmun, (modern-day Bahrain) in Ur's harbor.

ZAGROS MTS

TIGRIS

GREAT ZAB

LITTLE ZAB

Nineveh

Arbela

ASSYRIA

Ashur

DIYALA

M E S O P O T A M I A

EUPHRATES

TIGRIS

Jemdet Nasr

Babylon

Nippur

Isin

Umma

Lagash

Larsa

Ubaid

Ur

Eridu

SUMER

AKKAD

ELAM

Susa

TIGRIS

EUPHRATES

0 25 50 75 100 Kilometers

0 25 50 75 Miles

TRADE ROUTE TO INDIA

TRADE ROUTE TO DILMUN

PERSIAN GULF

Egypt—Life on the Nile

WITHOUT THE LIFE-GIVING WATERS of the Nile River, Egypt would be a desert and there would have been no Egyptian civilization. Many thousands of years ago, groups of hunters moved into the Nile valley. They found large numbers of animals, birds, and fish, as well as a reliable supply of water in the Nile River. They began to settle and, in about 5000 BCE, adopted farming as their way of life. As these farmers prospered, communities joined together to form two kingdoms—Upper (Southern) Egypt and Lower (Northern) Egypt.

Then, in about 3100 BCE, the king of Upper Egypt conquered the north and united the two kingdoms. Once the kingdoms were joined, Egyptian culture blossomed. Along with the Sumerians, the Egyptians were one of the first peoples to invent a system of writing. Their sculptors and painters produced many works of art and their architects built enormous temples and pyramids.

The Nile in flood

Every year each summer rains in the mountains at the Nile's source caused the river to overflow farther down in the flat valley. Farmers learned how to dig canals and basins to store the floodwater. Later in the year they guided this water onto the fields through ditches. If it was a "good Nile" the floods covered the land with a rich, black mud that fertilized the fields.

Foreign trade

Thanks to the annual flood, the Egyptians could grow more food than they needed. They sold the surplus abroad, trading with Canaan in the east, with Nubia and Punt to the south, and Libya to the west. Later they exchanged goods with Crete and Greece and with the Babylonian Empire. The Egyptians exported agricultural produce, linen, papyrus (a form of paper), and manufactured goods. They imported timber, incense, silver, horses, copper, tin, and wine. They also bought people to enslave them.

Boats on the river

The Nile River was Egypt's main highway, providing an easy and efficient means of transporting people and goods. Small boats were made of bundles of reeds lashed together. Bigger boats were made of wood held together with wooden pegs and ropes. The boats could be taken apart and carried across the Eastern Desert to the Red Sea, or around the great rocks, called cataracts, that blocked the Nile. They were then reassembled and put back into the water.

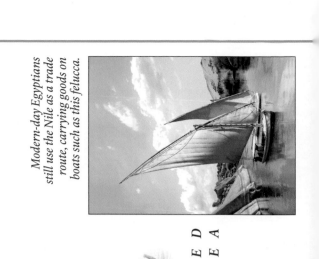

Modern-day Egyptians still use the Nile as a trade route, carrying goods on boats such as this felucca.

Horses, pottery, and enslaved people were imported from Canaan.

Cattle were driven to high ground to avoid the Nile floods.

Papyrus

Irrigation ditches divided Egyptian fields into small plots.

Plowing fields

Grain was stored in huge terra-cotta jars.

Harvesting grain

Fishing on the Nile

Date palms

MEDITERRANEAN SEA

TRADE ROUTE TO CANAAN

TRADE ROUTE TO LIBYA

NILE DELTA

Sais
Tanis
Avaris
Giza
Memphis
Saqqara
FAIYUM OASIS
Heracleopolis
Beni Hasan
El-Amarna
Abydos
Dendera
Coptos
Thebes
Armant

OVERLAND ROUTE TO COPPER AND TURQUOISE MINES

SINAI

RED SEA

TRADE ROUTE TO PUNT

EASTERN DESERT

WESTERN

E G Y P T

Fun and games

The Egyptians had many leisure activities. Nobles hunted in the deserts and the wild marshes of the Nile, either on foot or from chariots. Men from the lower classes of society took part in wrestling matches or water tournaments, where they tried to knock each other from boats into the river.

Storytellers, acrobats, musicians, and dancers were all popular entertainers.

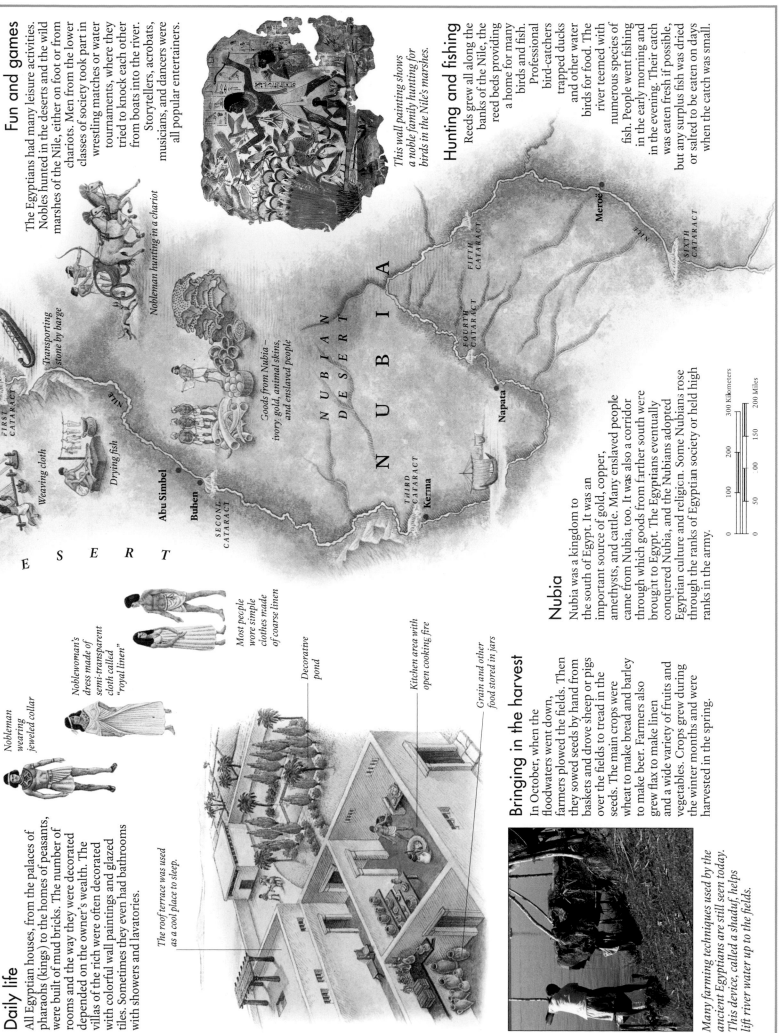

This wall painting shows a noble family hunting for birds in the Nile's marshes.

Nobleman hunting in a chariot

Transporting stone by barge

Weaving cloth

Drying fish

FIRST CATARACT

NILE

Abu Simbel

Buhen

SECOND CATARACT

Goods from Nubia – ivory, gold, animal skins, and enslaved people

Kerma

THIRD CATARACT

NUBIAN DESERT

N U B I A

Napata

FOURTH CATARACT

FIFTH CATARACT

Meroë

NILE

SIXTH CATARACT

Hunting and fishing

Reeds grew all along the banks of the Nile, the reed beds providing a home for many birds and fish. Professional bird-catchers trapped ducks and other water birds for food. The river teemed with numerous species of fish. People went fishing in the early morning and in the evening. Their catch was eaten fresh if possible, but any surplus fish was dried or salted to be eaten on days when the catch was small.

Nubia

Nubia was a kingdom to the south of Egypt. It was an important source of gold, copper, amethysts, and cattle. Many enslaved people came from Nubia, too. It was also a corridor through which goods from farther south were brought to Egypt. The Egyptians eventually conquered Nubia, and the Nubians adopted Egyptian culture and religion. Some Nubians rose through the ranks of Egyptian society or held high ranks in the army.

Scale bars:
300 Kilometers
200 Miles
0   100   200
0   50   100   150

Daily life

All Egyptian houses, from the palaces of pharaohs (kings) to the homes of peasants, were built of mud bricks. The number of rooms and the way they were decorated depended on the owner's wealth. The villas of the rich were often decorated with colorful wall paintings and glazed tiles. Sometimes they even had bathrooms with showers and lavatories.

Nobleman wearing jeweled collar

Noblewoman's dress made of semi-transparent cloth called "royal linen"

Most people wore simple clothes made of coarse linen

Decorative pond

Kitchen area with open cooking fire

Grain and other food stored in jars

The roof terrace was used as a cool place to sleep.

Bringing in the harvest

In October, when the floodwaters went down, farmers plowed the fields. Then they sowed seeds by hand from baskets and drove sheep or pigs over the fields to tread in the seeds. The main crops were wheat to make bread and barley to make beer. Farmers also grew flax to make linen and a wide variety of fruits and vegetables. Crops grew during the winter months and were harvested in the spring.

Many farming techniques used by the ancient Egyptians are still seen today. This device, called a shaduf, helps lift river water up to the fields.

D E S E R T

Egypt—Pharaohs and Pyramids

THE MOST IMPORTANT PERSON in Egypt was the pharaoh, or king. He was once thought to be so powerful that it was dangerous to touch him, even by accident. The Egyptians believed that when their king was seated on the throne holding the symbols of power, the spirit of the god Horus entered him and he became god on earth. He was responsible for Egypt's well-being and for ensuring the country was run as the gods intended.

The Egyptians believed in life after death. When a king died, his body was placed in a special tomb, called a pyramid, with clothes, furniture, jewelry, and personal belongings for use in the next world. The first pyramids had steps on the outside so that the king could climb them to join the gods. However, religious beliefs changed and pyramids became straight sided. Later kings were buried in highly decorated tombs cut into the rock of the cliffs in the Valley of the Kings to hide them from grave robbers.

The warrior pharaohs of the New Kingdom conquered the largest empire of their day. This map shows the extent of Egyptian rule in about 1400 BCE.

The rule of the pharaohs

Pharaohs ruled Egypt for about 3,000 years. Historians divide this long period of history into the Old, Middle, and New Kingdoms. As the king of Egypt was believed to be descended from the gods, it was difficult to know who was good enough to be his queen. He could have many wives, but his queen (known as Great Royal Wife) had to be royal, so the blood of the gods was not diluted. For this reason kings often married their sisters or a close female relative. Their eldest son became the next pharaoh.

One of the early pharaohs of the New Kingdom was Queen Hatshepsut. When her husband died she pushed her stepson Tuthmosis III aside and made herself "king" of Egypt.

The ankh, the Egyptian symbol of life, was carried as an amulet, or good luck charm.

KEY TO MAP

△ Pyramid

▦ Temple

▦ Tomb

▮ Obelisk

King Tutankhamun and Queen Ankhesenamun relax under the rays of the sun god.

Affairs of state

The king of Egypt had many roles. As head of the government he controlled the law, the army, and the cults of all the gods. At important festivals he performed the temple rituals in person so the people could see him as a god king. With his queen, he welcomed foreign princes bearing gifts. To help him govern, he had two chief ministers (for Upper and Lower Egypt) and an army of officials, scribes, and priests.

Anubis, jackal-headed guardian of the dead

The sun god as Khepri the scarab beetle

Horus, hawk-headed sky god

Thoth, god of wisdom, with his ibis head

Osiris, god of the dead

Homes of the gods

The Egyptians had a lot of gods and goddesses. Many were shown with a human body and the head of the bird or animal that represented its power. Huge, beautifully decorated temples were built as earthly homes for these gods, and statues of each were placed in sanctuaries and removed only for religious ceremonies. The greatest god in the New Kingdom was Amun, king of the gods. His temple at Karnak still stands.

The royal blue war helmet

The bow and arrow were often used.

Chariots were made of wood and bronze.

In the New Kingdom pharaohs rode into battle. Chariots were brought into Egypt by the Hyksos, invaders from the northeast.

Two decorated horses pulled each chariot.

The Egyptian army

In the Old and Middle Kingdoms, Egypt had only a small army of foot soldiers to protect its frontiers. In a national emergency, ordinary citizens could be called up for duty. In the New Kingdom, however, the horse and chariot were used for the first time and the army became a large, permanent force.

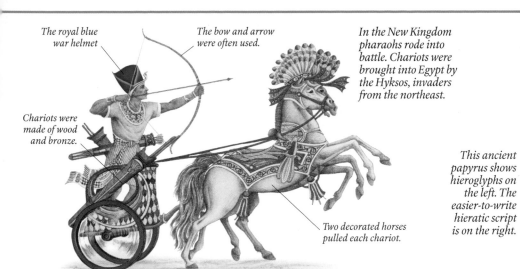

This ancient papyrus shows hieroglyphs on the left. The easier-to-write hieratic script is on the right.

The development of writing

In about 3300 BCE, the Egyptians invented a system of writing using picture signs that we call hieroglyphs. There were more than 700 signs. Hieroglyphic script took a long time to write, so a shorthand version, called hieratic, was started. Scripts were written on a kind of paper made from papyrus reed stems.

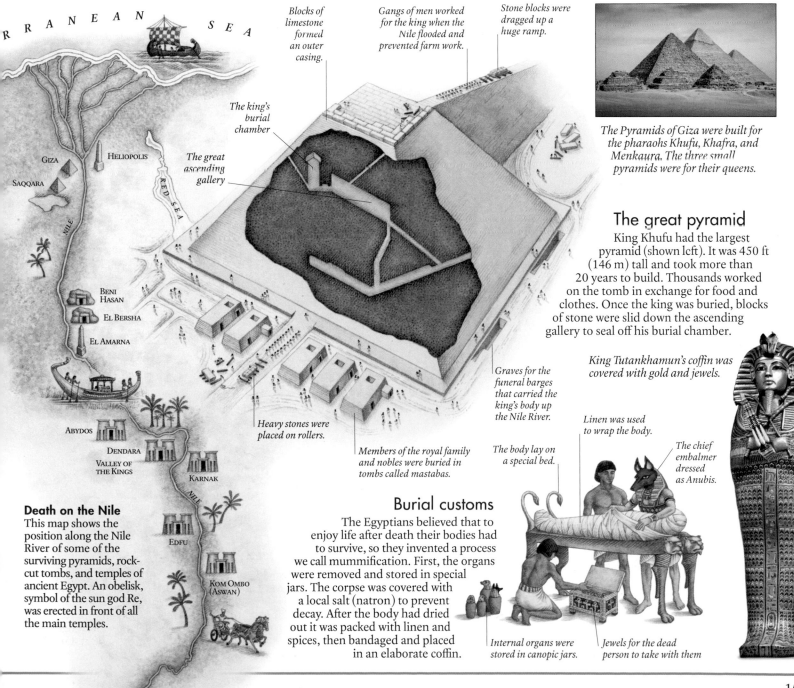

Blocks of limestone formed an outer casing.

Gangs of men worked for the king when the Nile flooded and prevented farm work.

Stone blocks were dragged up a huge ramp.

The king's burial chamber

The great ascending gallery

The Pyramids of Giza were built for the pharaohs Khufu, Khafra, and Menkaura. The three small pyramids were for their queens.

The great pyramid

King Khufu had the largest pyramid (shown left). It was 450 ft (146 m) tall and took more than 20 years to build. Thousands worked on the tomb in exchange for food and clothes. Once the king was buried, blocks of stone were slid down the ascending gallery to seal off his burial chamber.

Graves for the funeral barges that carried the king's body up the Nile River.

Heavy stones were placed on rollers.

Members of the royal family and nobles were buried in tombs called mastabas.

MEDITERRANEAN SEA

GIZA
HELIOPOLIS
SAQQARA
NILE
RED SEA
BENI HASAN
EL BERSHA
EL AMARNA
ABYDOS
DENDARA
VALLEY OF THE KINGS
KARNAK
NILE
EDFU
KOM OMBO (ASWAN)

Death on the Nile
This map shows the position along the Nile River of some of the surviving pyramids, rock-cut tombs, and temples of ancient Egypt. An obelisk, symbol of the sun god Re, was erected in front of all the main temples.

King Tutankhamun's coffin was covered with gold and jewels.

Linen was used to wrap the body.

The chief embalmer dressed as Anubis.

The body lay on a special bed.

Burial customs

The Egyptians believed that to enjoy life after death their bodies had to survive, so they invented a process we call mummification. First, the organs were removed and stored in special jars. The corpse was covered with a local salt (natron) to prevent decay. After the body had dried out it was packed with linen and spices, then bandaged and placed in an elaborate coffin.

Internal organs were stored in canopic jars.

Jewels for the dead person to take with them

Indus Valley Civilization

This statue from the city of Mohenjo-Daro is probably that of a priest. Some experts think the priests may also have been the kings.

ALONG THE VALLEY of the Indus River in modern-day India and Pakistan, another civilization had developed. For a while, in about 2500 BCE, it was one of the world's greatest civilizations. Successful farmers grew crops in the fertile soil along the river, and used its mud to make bricks for their buildings. Archaeologists have explored the remains of two large cities—at Mohenjo-Daro and Harappa. Both had populations of up to 40,000 people. Inside the city walls was a huge artificial hill made of mud and bricks. Perched on top, local rulers lived in a large fortress that overlooked the city.

Despite these achievements, this society died out in about 1500 BCE and many details of the Indus Valley people remain unknown. Experts have not been able to explain why this happened, nor have they managed to read the Indus Valley writing that could offer clues to the past.

Clean living

Wealthy Indus Valley families lived in comfortable houses built around courtyards. Stairs led to a flat roof where there was extra space to work and relax. Although there was not much furniture, the homes had wells for water and bathrooms with pipes that carried waste into the main drains. Cleanliness was obviously very important and bathing may have played a part in the religious rituals.

The Indus people used spears to kill animals for food. They may also have hunted for sport.

In about 1500 BCE, people called Indo-Aryans migrated into the Indus Valley.

HINDU KUSH

I N D U S

Mud was used to make bricks and pots.

• Mohenjo-Daro

The Great Bath at Mohenjo-Daro may have been used to cleanse and purify rulers and priests before religious ceremonies.

• Chanhu-Daro

Amri •

• Sutkagen-Dor

Farmers knew how to control flooding from the river, and divert the water to their crops.

Fishing nets were probably made from cotton strong enough to catch sea fish.

Inside a typical house in a Mohenjo-Daro street scene

The fortress, or citadel, where the important buildings were situated.

The roof was used for drying crops ready for storage.

Beds were probably made from simple wooden frames with woven leather strips.

A R A B I A N   S E A

Houses had separate toilets connected to the main drainage system.

A door opened onto the street but windows faced the courtyard for privacy.

Drains were laid under the streets. Workers climbed through inspection holes to clean them.

A wooden balcony overlooked a central courtyard.

Homes had their own wells.

TRADE ROUTE TO SUMER

Oxcarts with solid wooden wheels were used to transport goods overland.

H I M A L A Y A S

INDUS

JHELUM

CHENAB

TRADE ROUTE TO BACTRIA

RAVI

Harappa

SUTLEJ

The Indus Valley people were the first to grow cotton for weaving into cloth.

The government collected grain as a form of tax. It was stored in a huge granary on the citadel for times of famine.

V A L L E Y

Kalibangan

T H A R

D E S E R T

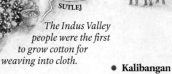

Craftworkers made stone seals with pictures of animals known to the people, such as humped bulls, elephants, and tigers. The seals show examples of the Indus Valley script.

This terra-cotta statue shows the mother goddess wearing an elaborate headdress. As the "mother of the world" she was believed to give the power of life to plants, animals, and humans.

The Mother Goddess

Judging from the number of statues that have been found, the Mother Goddess was hugely important to the Indus Valley people. She was probably worshipped in the home or in small local shrines, as no large temples have been found. There seems to have been a variety of beliefs among the people of the Indus Valley. Remains of fire altars suggest there were animal sacrifices. There was also a male god with horns who is shown seated on a throne and surrounded by animals. He may be an early version of the great god Shiva, who is known from later Hinduism.

Arts and crafts

Women liked to wear ornate necklaces, bangles, and earrings made from gold, silver, shells, and stones such as carnelian, a red-colored quartz. The Indus pottery was also of good quality and was often red with black geometric or flower designs. Stone carvers produced some remarkable pieces made from soapstone, a soft whitish stone with a "soapy" feel to it. Soapstone was also used to make the seals that merchants used to mark their property.

By land and sea

The people of the Indus were not entirely self-sufficient. They needed tin, which they mixed with copper to make bronze, and semiprecious stones for jewelry, which they imported overland from modern-day Afghanistan and Persia. The Indus traders also traveled overseas. Lothal had a brick-built harbor that merchant ships could enter at high tide through a special channel, unloading their goods into dockside warehouses. Traders paid with ivory, timber, cotton cloth, gems, and spices.

Oxcarts were once widely used to transport goods through the Indus Valley. They are still used in some countries.

Lothal

Rangpur

Merchants of the Indus Valley probably sailed from Lothal to Dilmun (modern Bahrain), where they met up with traders from Sumer.

End of an era

No one is really sure exactly what caused the decline of the Indus Valley civilization. Natural causes such as floods, droughts, or illness might have played a part. But the people themselves may have overused the land. As the population grew, they grazed more sheep and cows for food and clothes, and chopped down more timber for cooking and building. Overuse of the land may have ruined the soil so less food could be grown. The final blow may have been the arrival, in about 1500 BCE, of groups of people called Indo-Aryans who were seeking new homes.

G U L F   O F
C A M B A Y

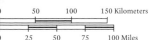

0   50   100   150 Kilometers

0   25   50   75   100 Miles

Europe—The Monument Builders

MASSIVE BLOCKS OF STONE still stand in a circle that forms the ancient monument of Stonehenge in southern England. From about 2500 BCE people across western Europe built large circles and long avenues of stones to honor their gods. They also dug great mounds of earth to mark the burial places of their dead. Experts believe the stone circles may have been used for religious ceremonies or to follow the movements of the sun and moon.

But while temples and cities were being built elsewhere in the world, Europeans preferred village life. Farming had spread to Europe sometime before 4000 BCE, with forests being cut down to provide wood for building houses and to clear the ground for growing crops. The discovery of tin, which workers mixed with copper to make bronze, provided stronger tools and weapons. This was the beginning of Bronze Age Europe.

Round huts had thatched roofs.

A palisade (fence) protected the village.

Food was stored in rooms on stilts to keep it from being eaten by rats.

Cattle were kept safe in pens inside the village.

Cutting wheat

Village life

Most people in Europe settled in small villages or lived on isolated farms. They built houses from locally sourced materials, such as wood and thatch, or stone and turf. Some houses, in Switzerland and northern Italy, had room for up to 50 people. Farmers grew wheat and barley and kept cattle, pigs, sheep, and goats. Apples, raspberries, plums, and strawberries grew wild. We know a lot about the food people ate from their garbage pits.

A local chief prepared for war with bronze weapons and armor.

Grain wo[s] ground between two stone[s] to make flour.

Setting up Stonehenge

Experts are not sure how Stonehenge was built. Construction began in about 3000 BCE, when workers dug a henge—a circular ditch and bank of earth—that enclosed a ring of pits. Around 2600 BCE a double circle of stones was added. About 200 years later these were replaced with a ring of huge upright stones (sarsens). By 2000 BCE the first stones had been restored to create a complex set of stone circles with the sarsens.

The arch is called a trilithon. This means "three stones" in Greek.

Men built a cradle of logs under each stone to raise and position it as a crossbeam on two sarsens.

A sarsen (upright) being raised into position. Its base stood in a pit.

One theory is that stones were lashed to a sled and pulled along, using logs as rollers.

Many of Europe's forests were cleared by farmers needing more land.

Tin was a valuable trading item. Much of it was mined in Spain.

Dead and buried

The monument builders believed in a life after death. Personal possessions, including pots and tools for the afterlife, have been found in their graves. Some men and women were buried under large earth mounds, known as barrows, with rich grave goods of gold and bronze. In about 1200 BCE a new culture, known as Urnfield, began to develop. When people died, they were cremated and their ashes placed in urns in cemeteries known as urnfields.

Funeral processions were held at the spectacular burial mound at Los Millares.

KEY TO MAP

- Stone avenue
- Stone circle
- Burial site
- Tin mine

```
0     100    200    300    400 Kilometers
|      |      |      |      |
0   50   100   150   200   250 Miles
```

Map labels

SHETLAND ISLANDS
Jarlshof
CALLANISH
HEBRIDES
SCOTLAND
NOR[TH] S[EA]
IRELAND
BALLYNOE
Mold
BRENIG
WALES
Fengate
ENGLAND
Runnymede
STONEHENGE
ISLES OF SCILLY
ATLANTIC OCEAN
KERNONEN
CARNAC
ER LANNIC
Aulnay-Planch[e]
SEINE
E[UROPE]
FRAN[CE]
GARONNE
Cortes de Navarra
EBRO
TAGUS
SPAIN
Los Millares
BALEARIC ISLANDS
MEDI[TERRANEAN]
AFRICA

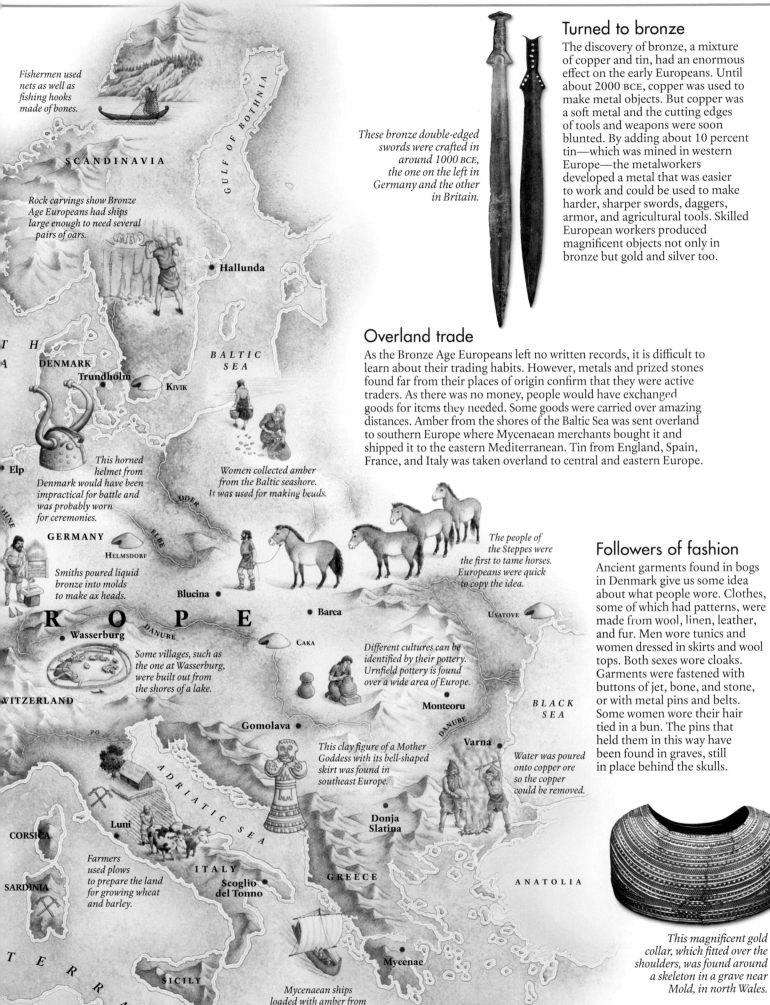

Fishermen used nets as well as fishing hooks made of bones.

SCANDINAVIA

GULF OF BOTHNIA

Rock carvings show Bronze Age Europeans had ships large enough to need several pairs of oars.

BALTIC SEA

• Hallunda

DENMARK
Trundholm
KIVIK

This horned helmet from Denmark would have been impractical for battle and was probably worn for ceremonies.

Elp

ODER

Women collected amber from the Baltic seashore. It was used for making beads.

RHINE

GERMANY
ELBE
HELMSDORF

Smiths poured liquid bronze into molds to make ax heads.

The people of the Steppes were the first to tame horses. Europeans were quick to copy the idea.

Blucina •

ROPE

DANUBE

• Barca

CAKA

USATOVE

Wasserburg •

Some villages, such as the one at Wasserburg, were built out from the shores of a lake.

WITZERLAND

Different cultures can be identified by their pottery. Urnfield pottery is found over a wide area of Europe.

Monteoru •

BLACK SEA

PO

Gomolava •

DANUBE

Varna •

This clay figure of a Mother Goddess with its bell-shaped skirt was found in southeast Europe.

Water was poured onto copper ore so the copper could be removed.

ADRIATIC SEA

CORSICA

Luni •

Donja Slatina •

Farmers used plows to prepare the land for growing wheat and barley.

SARDINIA

ITALY
Scoglio del Tonno •

GREECE

ANATOLIA

SICILY

Mycenae •

Mycenaean ships loaded with amber from the Baltic Sea sailed to the eastern Mediterranean.

TERRANEAN SEA

MALTA

CRETE

Turned to bronze

The discovery of bronze, a mixture of copper and tin, had an enormous effect on the early Europeans. Until about 2000 BCE, copper was used to make metal objects. But copper was a soft metal and the cutting edges of tools and weapons were soon blunted. By adding about 10 percent tin—which was mined in western Europe—the metalworkers developed a metal that was easier to work and could be used to make harder, sharper swords, daggers, armor, and agricultural tools. Skilled European workers produced magnificent objects not only in bronze but gold and silver too.

These bronze double-edged swords were crafted in around 1000 BCE, the one on the left in Germany and the other in Britain.

Overland trade

As the Bronze Age Europeans left no written records, it is difficult to learn about their trading habits. However, metals and prized stones found far from their places of origin confirm that they were active traders. As there was no money, people would have exchanged goods for items they needed. Some goods were carried over amazing distances. Amber from the shores of the Baltic Sea was sent overland to southern Europe where Mycenaean merchants bought it and shipped it to the eastern Mediterranean. Tin from England, Spain, France, and Italy was taken overland to central and eastern Europe.

Followers of fashion

Ancient garments found in bogs in Denmark give us some idea about what people wore. Clothes, some of which had patterns, were made from wool, linen, leather, and fur. Men wore tunics and women dressed in skirts and wool tops. Both sexes wore cloaks. Garments were fastened with buttons of jet, bone, and stone, or with metal pins and belts. Some women wore their hair tied in a bun. The pins that held them in this way have been found in graves, still in place behind the skulls.

This magnificent gold collar, which fitted over the shoulders, was found around a skeleton in a grave near Mold, in north Wales.

Minoans and Mycenaeans

ALMOST FOUR THOUSAND YEARS AGO, the Mediterranean island of Crete was the center of Europe's first great civilization. The island's largest settlement was Knossos, which boasted a brilliantly decorated palace housing the ruling family. The Cretans were sailors who grew rich by trading with other Mediterranean peoples. They developed their own way of life, which included an extraordinary bull-leaping ceremony. We call these people the Minoans, after a legendary Cretan king named Minos.

The Minoans were very successful. But in about 1450 BCE, warriors from mainland Greece took over. These invaders were Mycenaeans, named after the city of Mycenae where the remains of their civilization were first discovered, and they seem to have been a warlike people. They adopted many of the Minoan ways of life. Both civilizations spoke an early form of the Greek language and believed in the importance of female gods.

Island of palaces

Archaeologists have discovered the remains of four imposing palaces on Crete—at Knossos, Mallia, Zakros, and Phaistos. The largest, at Knossos, was five floors high in places and with 1,300 rooms. The royal rooms were decorated with colorful wall paintings, called frescoes, depicting court life and sea scenes such as leaping dolphins. The palace complex was built around a central courtyard used for religious ceremonies. Knossos had its own water supply and drainage system.

Mycenaean palaces were built on hilltops and protected by high walls made of huge stone blocks. We call these Cyclopean walls, after the one-eyed giant Cyclops who legend says built the walls.

Grapes were used to make wine. They were put in tubs and trampled to extract the juice.

Harvesting grain

Minoans and Mycenaeans made intricate gold jewelry such as this earring.

Hunting wild boar

Iolkos

Orchomenos

Gla

Thebes

G R E E C E

Athens

A Mycenaean warrior wore a suit of bronze armor and a helmet decorated with boar's tusks.

Early Mycenaean kings were buried in shaft graves protected by a stone circle.

Mycenae

Tiryns

Pylos

Women knocked olives from the trees, and men crushed them in a stone press to extract oil for cooking and lighting.

In about 1450 BCE Mycenaeans sailed to Crete and took over the island.

TRADE ROUTE TO SICILY

M E D

I O N I A N   S E A

When archaeologists found the throne room, they discovered the oldest throne in Europe.

Light wells allowed daylight and cool air to filter into the palace.

Bull leaping probably took place in the central courtyard.

Cretan townhouses had two or three floors, windows, and a little room on the roof.

Reconstruction of palace at Knossos

The walls were built of local limestone.

Wooden pillars were painted in red and blue.

The Minoans grew olive trees in the countryside around the palace.

Legend says that when the Greeks gave up their siege of Troy, they left a huge wooden horse. When the Trojans brought the horse into their city, Greek warriors hidden inside its hollow body climbed out and opened the gates of Troy. The main army charged in and conquered the city.

• **Troy**

The Trojan War

The legend of the Trojan War is probably based on battles that took place in Mycenaean times. It tells of Paris, Prince of Troy, who ran off with Helen, Queen of Sparta. To get her back from Troy, Helen's husband, Menelaus, and his brother, Agamemnon of Mycenae, called all the kings together and set off with an army. After a 10-year siege, the Mycenaeans eventually captured the city using a wooden horse. Paris and most of the Trojan men were slain and Helen was sent back to her husband, Menelaus.

A S I A   M I N O R

A E G E A N   S E A

Golden Mycenae

The Mycenaeans lived in hilltop cities, such as Tiryns, Gla, and Mycenae itself. At Mycenae, the royal family lived in a beautiful palace on a specially fortified hilltop called a citadel. Anyone who worked for the palace, such as officials, scribes, and craftworkers, lived in the upper town between the palace and the defensive wall. Most people, however, were farmers or merchants.

When a Mycenaean king died, he was laid out in royal robes and a gold mask was placed over his face. This mask was found in a grave at Mycenae.

Fishermen caught tuna, mackerel, mullet, and octopus.

Miletus

Merchants from the Greek colony of Miletus traded with the Hittites.

Written records

In Minoan and Mycenaean Greece, the king controlled the economy. People paid taxes in the form of wheat, olive oil, pottery, and metalwork, which were used to pay the army, officials, and craftworkers. Any surplus was traded overseas to buy tin, gold, and ivory. Both the Minoans and Mycenaeans kept written records. The Minoans used a form of writing we call Linear A. Later, the Mycenaeans developed Linear B. So far, experts can only understand Linear B.

Mycenaean pottery, ivory, and bronze swords were found on a vessel that sank off the coast at Ulu Burun.

In about 1450 BCE, a volcano erupted on the island of Thera, modern Santorini. It blew the island apart.

I T E R R A N E A N   S E A

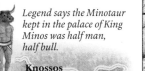

Legend says the Minotaur kept in the palace of King Minos was half man, half bull.

Knossos

Mallia

R E T E

Phaistos

Zakro

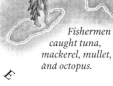

Oil, grain, and wine were stored in huge pottery jars called pithoi.

Minoan men and women were trained to leap over the backs of charging bulls as part of a religious ceremony.

TRADE ROUTE FROM EGYPT

The goddess rules

For both the Minoans and Mycenaeans, the goddess was the most important religious figure. She appeared in many different forms—as a snake, a goddess of the sea, and a goddess of caves who looked after women during childbirth. Shrines were built within palaces and in the countryside where people could leave offerings of sweet oils, honey, or wine. The Minoans also believed that the bull was a sacred animal, and decorated their palaces and pottery with images of its horns.

Fish and other sea creatures were popular pottery designs, reflecting the importance of the sea to the Minoans.

0	25	50	75 Kilometers
0		25	50 Miles

Canaan— Land of Plenty

CANAAN is the ancient name for the land at the eastern end of the Mediterranean, in what is now Israel and Lebanon, and part of Syria and Jordan. It was to become a land fought over by many people. In about 2000 BCE, this land boasted huge cedar forests in the north, and rich soil for farming around the Jordan and Orontes rivers. Canaan also lay at the meeting point between Africa and Asia, a perfect position to control trade between the two. Many great empire builders of the day, from the Egyptians to the Mesopotamians, fought for control here. Even tribes wandering on the desert fringe dreamed of settling in Canaan's farmlands.

Much of what we know about life in Canaan comes from texts written on clay tablets. Tablets found in the city of Ugarit help us understand Canaanite religion. They were written after 1700 BCE, when the Canaanites started to use a new way of writing—an alphabet with only 27 letters. This was easier to use than hieroglyphs and cuneiform, and formed the basis of the alphabet that we use today.

The Egyptians often had to send their army to control the empire they had won.

This piece of carved ivory from Megiddo shows a Canaanite king with a row of prisoners.

Hittites, warlike people from what is now Turkey (Türkiye), fought the Egyptians for control of Canaan.

Carchemish

The Mitanni from northern Mesopotamia added parts of Canaan to their empire for a while.

● **Aleppo**

Rulers of Canaan's many rival kingdoms lived in luxurious palaces in well-defended cities.

EUPHRATES

Ugarit ●

ORONTES

Egyptian pharaoh Tuthmosis III conquered areas as far north as modern-day Syria. For sport, he hunted elephants on the plains.

Arvad ●

The tall cedar trees, grown in what is now Lebanon, were felled and exported.

Trading ship

TO MYCENAE

TO EGYPT

C A N A A N

● **Byblos**

Harvesting wheat and grinding grain for bread and beer making

Tyre ●

Guards kept a close watch over vineyards near the bustling city of Hazor.

Hazor ●

Megiddo ●

SEA OF GALILEE

Priests sacrificed goats at the "high place" in Megiddo.

Nomads grazed sheep and goats on the fringes of Canaan. Some nomads became mercenary soldiers, some became bandits.

Jericho ●

JORDAN

A watchtower protected Jericho's earliest town. The city was destroyed in about 1560 BCE by Egyptians campaigning against the Hyksos people.

Jerusalem ●
Lachish ●

Hebron ●

DEAD SEA

| 0 | 25 | 50 | 75 | 100 Kilometers |

| 0 | 20 | 40 | 60 | 80 Miles |

This vase, found at Jericho, was made in about 1700 BCE.

Making a living

By 1500 BCE, Canaan was a land of city-states, each city and its surrounding villages ruled by its own king. Merchants, particularly at the great port of Byblos, took wood, silver, and ivory across the Mediterranean Sea to Egypt and Mycenae in Greece. Artists made fine jewelry and decorated pots. But farmers were the backbone of the community.

Worship in high places

The chief god in Canaan was El, who ruled the sky. But the most popular god was Hadad, better known as Baal, the weather god. Gods were served by priests and priestesses in richly decorated temples. They were also worshipped at sites on hilltops, known as "high places," where animals were sacrificed in front of pillars into which priests believed the divine spirits had entered.

This bronze statuette shows the Canaanite god Baal.

The city of Jericho

Jericho is one of the world's oldest towns. In about 8000 BCE, hunters and gatherers settled there because of the reliable supply of food and water. They built houses of mud brick and took up farming. Over the years they grew rich and built stone walls and watchtowers around the town to protect themselves and their wealth. Jericho's wealth may have come from trading salt and bitumen (asphalt) from the Dead Sea.

Kingdoms of the Hebrews

ACCORDING TO THE BIBLE, the nomadic Hebrew tribes from the land around Canaan were forced to work for the pharaohs in Egypt. They escaped from slavery and returned to conquer Canaan, which they believed had been promised to them by their god. But they had rivals. Egyptian records show that in about 1200 BCE the eastern Mediterranean was threatened by fierce invaders known as the Sea Peoples. One group, the Peleset (from which we get the name Palestine), settled in southern Canaan. In the Bible, the Peleset are called the Philistines.

For almost 200 years the Philistines and Hebrews lived side by side. But in about 1020 BCE the Hebrew tribes united against their old foes and established the kingdom of Israel. The new kingdom prospered under the rule of three great kings, Saul, David, and Solomon. When Solomon died in 922 BCE, squabbles between north and south split the kingdom in two, with Israel in the north and Judah in the south. The people of Judah later became known as Jews.

Solomon's kingdom

King Solomon reigned in about 960–922 BCE, and is remembered as a wise king. Although it was his father, David, who defeated the Philistines and established Jerusalem as his capital, Israel grew rich under Solomon. He stayed on good terms with his neighbors and even married an Egyptian princess. He kept an army so he could control the major trade routes and collect taxes and payments of gold. The profits were used to build the first temple of the Hebrews.

Ancient Jewish texts, now called the Dead Sea Scrolls, were found in 1947 in a cave at Qumran, shown above.

Most Hebrews became farmers. They grew wheat, barley, figs, nuts, pomegranates, and melons.

In 721 BCE, Sargon II, king of Assyria, destroyed Samaria, then Israel's capital.

The Bible tells how a shepherd boy, David, killed the Philistine champion, Goliath, with a stone.

The Hebrews lived in four-roomed houses.

MEDITERRANEAN SEA

PHOENICIA

SEA OF GALILEE

Megiddo

Samaria

ISRAEL

JORDAN

Jericho

Jerusalem

AMMON

Bethlehem

Qumran

JUDAH

DEAD SEA

Masada

Beersheba

MOAB

PHILISTIA

The Sea Peoples came from the islands and coasts of the northeast Mediterranean.

The Romans took the hilltop fortress of Masada in 74 CE. The defending Jews killed themselves rather than be taken prisoner.

One queen of Sabaea (Sheba) in southern Arabia is said to have visited King Solomon to test his wisdom.

EDOM

According to the Bible, the prophet Moses led the Hebrews from Egypt back into Canaan.

Ezion-Geber

This coin depicts King Antiochus IV, whose family took Judah from the Greeks. His attacks on the Jewish religion sparked off a revolt in 168 BCE.

RED SEA

SINAI

Trading ship

Copper was exported from the port of Ezion-Geber.

ARABIA

TO INDIA

0	25	50	75	100 Kilometers

0	20	40	60	80 Miles

The holiest part of the temple was paneled with wood inlaid with gold.

Main hall lined with cedar wood

Solomon's Temple

Bronze columns called Jachin and Boaz

The Ark of the Covenant was guarded by two golden cherubim.

Limestone walls

Religious texts and temples

The Hebrews were unusual among ancient peoples because they worshipped only one god, Yahweh. The laws of their religion and their history were gathered into a collection of books, now known to Christians as the Old Testament of the Bible. Solomon built a temple in Jerusalem to house the Ark of the Covenant, a box containing two tablets on which were written the Ten Commandments. The temple became the focus of Hebrew religious life.

Jerusalem under seige

The city of Jerusalem was under constant threat—from Assyrians, Babylonians, Persians, Greeks, and Romans. In 37 BCE, the Romans appointed Herod the Great as king. He and his successors were unpopular with their Jewish subjects and discontent led to several revolts, savagely put down by the Romans. Most Jews were forced to leave.

Phoenicians—Rulers of the Sea

ADVENTUROUS PHOENICIAN SAILORS explored the lands around the Mediterranean Sea. Their ships carried cedar wood, brightly colored glass, ivory, and purple-dyed cloth to trade with others. By about 700 BCE they had settled colonies on Malta, Sicily, and Sardinia, and as far away as Spain. Their most famous colony was at Carthage in Africa. The Phoenicians were descended from the Canaanites who lived along the eastern edge of the Mediterranean Sea. Their main cities were Arvad, Byblos, Berytus (Beirut), Sidon, and Tyre, in modern Lebanon. In about 1200 BCE the area was thrown into chaos by the arrival of the Sea Peoples and the collapse of the Mycenaean world. The Canaanites were quick to take over as the leading trading nation of the Mediterranean world. In their new role, we call them Phoenicians.

By 1000 BCE, the Phoenicians had produced a simple alphabet. It had 22 letters, all consonants. Vowels were added later by the Greeks to form the alphabet we use today.

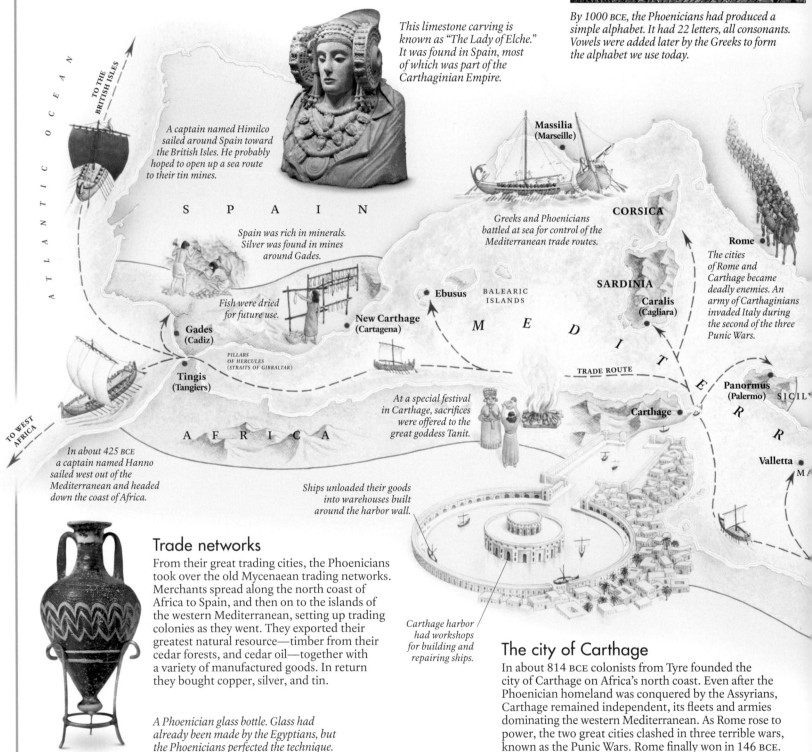

This limestone carving is known as "The Lady of Elche." It was found in Spain, most of which was part of the Carthaginian Empire.

A captain named Himilco sailed around Spain toward the British Isles. He probably hoped to open up a sea route to their tin mines.

TO THE BRITISH ISLES

ATLANTIC OCEAN

S P A I N

Spain was rich in minerals. Silver was found in mines around Gades.

Fish were dried for future use.

Gades (Cadiz)

PILLARS OF HERCULES (STRAITS OF GIBRALTAR)

Tingis (Tangiers)

Ebusus

New Carthage (Cartagena)

BALEARIC ISLANDS

Massilia (Marseille)

Greeks and Phoenicians battled at sea for control of the Mediterranean trade routes.

CORSICA

SARDINIA

Caralis (Cagliara)

Rome

The cities of Rome and Carthage became deadly enemies. An army of Carthaginians invaded Italy during the second of the three Punic Wars.

M E D I T E R R

TRADE ROUTE

Panormus (Palermo)   SICIL

A F R I C A

At a special festival in Carthage, sacrifices were offered to the great goddess Tanit.

Carthage

Valletta

M A

TO WEST AFRICA

In about 425 BCE a captain named Hanno sailed west out of the Mediterranean and headed down the coast of Africa.

Ships unloaded their goods into warehouses built around the harbor wall.

Carthage harbor had workshops for building and repairing ships.

Trade networks

From their great trading cities, the Phoenicians took over the old Mycenaean trading networks. Merchants spread along the north coast of Africa to Spain, and then on to the islands of the western Mediterranean, setting up trading colonies as they went. They exported their greatest natural resource—timber from their cedar forests, and cedar oil—together with a variety of manufactured goods. In return they bought copper, silver, and tin.

A Phoenician glass bottle. Glass had already been made by the Egyptians, but the Phoenicians perfected the technique.

The city of Carthage

In about 814 BCE colonists from Tyre founded the city of Carthage on Africa's north coast. Even after the Phoenician homeland was conquered by the Assyrians, Carthage remained independent, its fleets and armies dominating the western Mediterranean. As Rome rose to power, the two great cities clashed in three terrible wars, known as the Punic Wars. Rome finally won in 146 BCE.

Ships and sailing

The Phoenicians had two kinds of ships. Their long, fast war galleys were powered by oars and sails and had vicious iron rams on the prows to hole enemy ships. The trading vessels, like the one shown here, were much wider. Phoenician sailors took advantage of seasonal winds, setting out with one favorable wind and returning with another. The Egyptian pharaoh Necho II hired expert Phoenician sailors to undertake a voyage of exploration around Africa. It took three years.

Sailors climbed the mast to keep watch. Phoenician sailors aimed to sail within sight of land.

A Phoenician trading ship had a central, single mast and a square sail.

The steersman stood at the stern to guide the ship using two great oars.

Steering oars

The ship's owner prays for good weather.

A tar coating made the ship watertight.

Most cargo was stored belowdecks and lashed firmly into place.

The cargo often included pottery jars full of cedar oil, glass jars, and copper ingots.

Crafts

In any Phoenician city there were craftworkers making goods for everyday use—pottery, tools, fancy metalwork, and drinking goblets. The Phoenicians were smart, quick to copy and adapt the techniques and art styles of others to their own advantage. But there were some crafts at which they excelled. They were expert ship builders. Their carpenters made wonderful furniture—beds, chairs, and chests inlaid with carved ivory—which they traded abroad. Phoenician glass was much in demand, as was an expensive purple cloth (later used by the Romans to clothe their emperors).

Grotesque masks have been found in Phoenician and Carthaginian graves. They may have been thought to drive off evil spirits.

Life on the land

Phoenicia was lucky to have fertile farmlands both along the coast and in the inland valleys. This allowed farmers to grow all the food they needed. Many Phoenicians, however, lived in coastal cities and worked as merchants, sailors, or craftworkers. The cities had defensive walls and the kings lived in luxurious palaces. Houses were cool and airy. Assyrian carvings show that palms and fruit trees grew in and around the cities, and that larger houses had roof gardens.

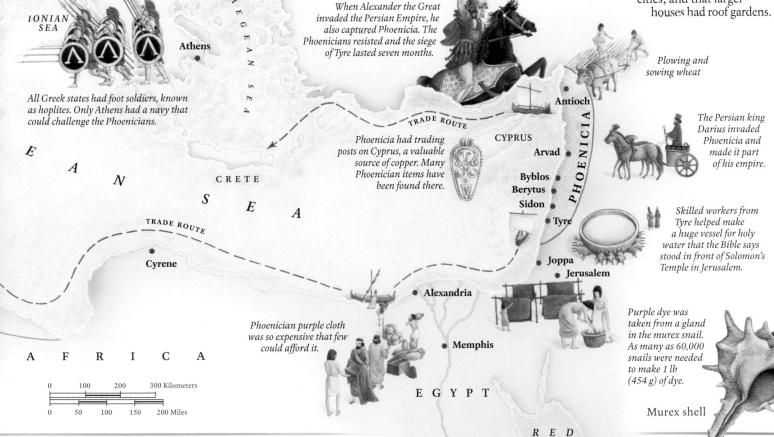

When Alexander the Great invaded the Persian Empire, he also captured Phoenicia. The Phoenicians resisted and the siege of Tyre lasted seven months.

All Greek states had foot soldiers, known as hoplites. Only Athens had a navy that could challenge the Phoenicians.

Phoenicia had trading posts on Cyprus, a valuable source of copper. Many Phoenician items have been found there.

Plowing and sowing wheat

The Persian king Darius invaded Phoenicia and made it part of his empire.

Skilled workers from Tyre helped make a huge vessel for holy water that the Bible says stood in front of Solomon's Temple in Jerusalem.

Phoenician purple cloth was so expensive that few could afford it.

Purple dye was taken from a gland in the murex snail. As many as 60,000 snails were needed to make 1 lb (454 g) of dye.

Murex shell

GREECE

ANATOLIA

IONIAN SEA

Athens

AEGEAN SEA

CRETE

TRADE ROUTE

CYPRUS

PHOENICIA

Antioch

Arvad

Byblos
Berytus
Sidon
Tyre

Joppa
Jerusalem

TRADE ROUTE

Cyrene

Alexandria

Memphis

AFRICA

EGYPT

0   100   200   300 Kilometers

0   50   100   150   200 Miles

RED SEA

NILE

25

Babylon—Gate of the Gods

BABYLON WAS A MAGNIFICENT CITY. It stood on the banks of the Euphrates River and was protected by walls so wide that two rows of four-horse chariots could ride along the top. The name Babylon means "gate of the gods" and the most impressive way into the city was through the Ishtar Gate. This grand entrance was decorated with brilliant blue tiles and figures of bulls and dragons. Beyond the gate a wide avenue, called the Processional Way, led to the city's center and the temple ziggurat dedicated to the chief god, Marduk. Nearby were the Hanging Gardens, one of the Seven Wonders of the Ancient World.

Babylon first became powerful under the rule of King Hammurabi (c.1792–1750 BCE). For many years it was the capital of Mesopotamia and a center of learning. But hundreds of years of invasions by Kassites, Chaldeans, and Assyrians almost destroyed it. Not until the reign of King Nebuchadnezzar II (605–562 BCE) did Babylon rise again to become the greatest city of its day.

The Hittite army crossed the Taurus Mountains and plundered Babylon in about 1595 BCE.

Hammurabi and the law

In about 1792 BCE a young man named Hammurabi, from an Amorite tribe, inherited the Babylonian throne. Hammurabi conquered all of Sumer and Akkad. We call the new kingdom Babylonia after its capital city, Babylon. One of his achievements was to establish a new code, setting out laws and penalties covering family, property, slaves, and wages. The phrases "an eye for an eye" and "a tooth for a tooth" come from these ancient law codes.

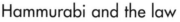

King Hammurabi's law code was engraved on a stone pillar (a stela). This section shows Hammurabi standing before Shamash, god of the sun and justice.

Kassites and Chaldeans

After Hammurabi's death, people we call Kassites set up a new dynasty in Babylon. They were mountain people and they ruled Babylonia successfully from 1595 BCE to 1155 BCE. In about 900 BCE, tribesmen known as Chaldeans settled in the coastal marshes of what had been Sumer. They fought for their freedom against the new Assyrian rulers of Babylonia. By 625 BCE, Nabopolassar, leader of the Chaldeans, had driven the Assyrians out and become king of Babylonia.

A Chaldean stone slab from the Temple of Marduk in Babylon, carved to commemorate a father and son.

The wise men

In Babylon, only boys went to school. They first learned to read and write the 500 or so different signs of their script, and went on to study literature, astronomy, and mathematics. Babylonians, like the Sumerians before them, based their mathematics on units of 60. From this, we get our 60 minutes in an hour and 360 degrees in a circle. They also studied the stars and planets. Several of the names used by Babylonian astronomers, such as the Twins (Gemini) and Capricorn, are still used to describe constellations.

This clay tablet shows a map of the world as the Babylonians saw it. The outer circle marks the ocean with the known world in the center.

In 597 BCE King Jehoiachin and 10,000 leading citizens of Jerusalem were carried off into captivity in Babylon.

The missing king

King Nabonidus (556–539 BCE) was the last king of Babylonia and a bit of a mystery. He was devoted to the moon god, Sin, and restored many temples. However, he was unpopular because he could not sort out the economic problems left by earlier kings. Curiously, and without warning, he moved to the oasis of Tayma in the Arabian Desert, leaving his son Belshazzar in charge. He stayed away for 10 years, but no one knows why. By the time he returned, the Persian king Cyrus the Great had captured Babylon.

TAURU

MEDITERRANEAN SEA

Byblos

Damascus

Tyre

Samaria

JORDAN

ISRAEL
Jerusalem

JUDAH

DEAD
SEA

RED
SEA

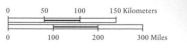

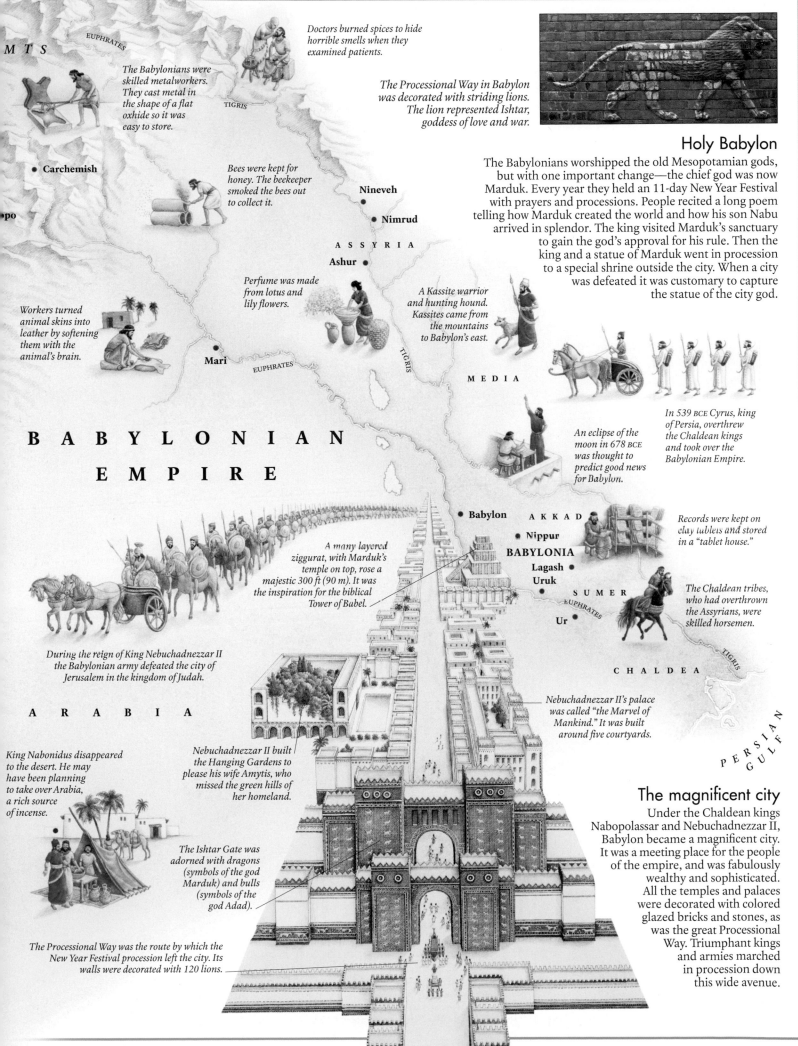

The Babylonians were skilled metalworkers. They cast metal in the shape of a flat oxhide so it was easy to store.

Doctors burned spices to hide horrible smells when they examined patients.

The Processional Way in Babylon was decorated with striding lions. The lion represented Ishtar, goddess of love and war.

Bees were kept for honey. The beekeeper smoked the bees out to collect it.

Workers turned animal skins into leather by softening them with the animal's brain.

Perfume was made from lotus and lily flowers.

A Kassite warrior and hunting hound. Kassites came from the mountains to Babylon's east.

Holy Babylon

The Babylonians worshipped the old Mesopotamian gods, but with one important change—the chief god was now Marduk. Every year they held an 11-day New Year Festival with prayers and processions. People recited a long poem telling how Marduk created the world and how his son Nabu arrived in splendor. The king visited Marduk's sanctuary to gain the god's approval for his rule. Then the king and a statue of Marduk went in procession to a special shrine outside the city. When a city was defeated it was customary to capture the statue of the city god.

An eclipse of the moon in 678 BCE was thought to predict good news for Babylon.

In 539 BCE Cyrus, king of Persia, overthrew the Chaldean kings and took over the Babylonian Empire.

A many layered ziggurat, with Marduk's temple on top, rose a majestic 300 ft (90 m). It was the inspiration for the biblical Tower of Babel.

Records were kept on clay tablets and stored in a "tablet house."

The Chaldean tribes, who had overthrown the Assyrians, were skilled horsemen.

During the reign of King Nebuchadnezzar II the Babylonian army defeated the city of Jerusalem in the kingdom of Judah.

Nebuchadnezzar II's palace was called "the Marvel of Mankind." It was built around five courtyards.

King Nabonidus disappeared to the desert. He may have been planning to take over Arabia, a rich source of incense.

Nebuchadnezzar II built the Hanging Gardens to please his wife Amytis, who missed the green hills of her homeland.

The Ishtar Gate was adorned with dragons (symbols of the god Marduk) and bulls (symbols of the god Adad).

The Processional Way was the route by which the New Year Festival procession left the city. Its walls were decorated with 120 lions.

The magnificent city

Under the Chaldean kings Nabopolassar and Nebuchadnezzar II, Babylon became a magnificent city. It was a meeting place for the people of the empire, and was fabulously wealthy and sophisticated. All the temples and palaces were decorated with colored glazed bricks and stones, as was the great Processional Way. Triumphant kings and armies marched in procession down this wide avenue.

27

Assyrians— Kings of Conquest

THE ASSYRIANS had to fight to survive. They originally lived in the hills around the Tigris River, in what is now northern Iraq, but were surrounded by people after their land. Until around 2000 BCE, the kings of Sumer and Akkad controlled Assyria. It was finally taken over by invaders from the southwest, which allowed the Assyrians to break free. Over the years, the Assyrians tried to extend their land but always failed. Then, in the 9th century BCE, came triumph. Under orders from their chief god, Ashur, the Assyrian kings began to conquer nearby kingdoms, succeeding without thought for human life. Defeated people were marched off to labor as slaves. By 612 BCE, the empire was too large to control and was defeated by an army of Babylonians and Medes (warriors from Persia).

Power of the kings

The Assyrian kings had titles such as "King of the Universe" and "Great King." They believed they were chosen by the gods to bring wealth and were in charge of their subjects. But a king also had to serve the gods—they were responsible for the priests and temples, and took the lead in key religious events. At one ceremony the high priest had to slap the king to remind him he was only a servant of the gods.

This wall carving is from the northwest palace at Nimrud, of King Ashurnasirpal II (883–859 BCE).

The map shows the extent of the Assyrian Empire in about 600 BCE.

Life at court

The Assyrians built beautiful cities. Their earliest capital was at Ashur, named after the god, but King Sennacherib (704–681 BCE) made Nineveh his headquarters. The palace was decorated with glazed tiles and stone carvings telling of the king's conquests. Inside there were at least 80 large rooms, including a library. Some kings had parks where they kept lions, leopards, bears, and elephants.

King Ashurbanipal (668–627 BCE) celebrates victory over the Elamites with Queen Ashursharrat at Nineveh.

Native princes ruled in Egypt, but Assyrian officials kept an eye on them.

Stone carvings of famous battles decorated the palace walls. This scene shows the army attacking a town in Egypt.

Wood from the tall cedar trees of Lebanon was used for building boats

Defeated people were taken into captivity.

The capture of Lachish by King Sennacherib

On the warpath

Military campaigns were planned in detail, with the king often leading his men into battle. Most of the army was made up of foot soldiers who did the dangerous fighting. They used bows, swords, slings, spears, and battle axes, and carried shields to protect themselves. When the army came home after a successful battle, there was a grand procession through the city to the temple where the king reported the good news to the god.

U R A R T U

Local tribes formed the kindom of Urartu to defend themselves against Assyrian attacks.

The Assyrians needed thousands of horses to keep their army moving.

LAKE VAN

M T S

TIGRIS

Workers carved great statues from local stone.

• Haran

Assyrian kings showed off their skill at royal lion hunts.

Khorsabad

Nineveh •
Nimrud •

GREAT ZAB

Arbela

Medes joined with Babylon to destroy the Assyrian Empire.

A S S Y R I A

LITTLE ZAB

Ashur •

Symbol of the chief god, Ashur

S S Y R I A N

M E D I A

Harvesting barley

E M P I R E

Assyrian wealth

The Assyrians took the riches they wanted from lands that had been defeated by the army. They already had a good source of local stone for building, but they also needed supplies of metal to make weapons and tools, timber to build boats, horses for their army, and food for the soldiers. Every year, as a token of submission to their Assyrian masters, conquered people had to pay tribute of any goods the Assyrians wanted. These demands were not popular, and the army often had to use force to make people pay.

Country life

The rolling hills of the Assyrian homeland were fertile, thanks to regular winter rains. The Assyrians dug ditches to irrigate their fields, and built aqueducts to carry water to their cities. The main crops were barley, sesame, and vegetables, and the Assyrian farmers kept sheep, goats, and cattle. Summers were warm enough to grow grapes, which were used to make wine. As the empire grew, the Assyrians demanded more food from defeated peoples. This allowed local farmers to become lazy and neglect their fields.

A shepherd with his sheep in modern-day Iraq. Many farmers today tend flocks in the same way as farmers of ancient times.

The palace at Nimrud had great stone monsters, symbols of power, to guard the doors to the throne room. The monsters had the bodies of lions or bulls with wings, and bearded human faces.

The Assyrians often cut down the orchards of rebel subjects.

Ziggurat at Babylon

Babylon • • Nippur

Susa •

People from defeated cities were often hung on poles as a warning to others.

B A B Y L O N I A

E L A M

• Uruk

EUPHRATES

Ur •

Soldiers crossed rivers on inflated goatskins.

TIGRIS

0   50   100   150   200 Kilometers
0 25 50 75 100 125 Miles

Men of war

Originally the army was made up of Assyrian farmers, who fought if not needed on their farms. As the empire grew, King Tiglath-pileser III (745–727 BCE) set up a permanent army made up of thousands of men taken from conquered lands. They were well trained and used wooden siege machines to attack enemy cities.

Babylonians plotting against Assyria hid in the marshes.

P E R S I A N
G U L F

TRADE ROUTE TO ARABIA

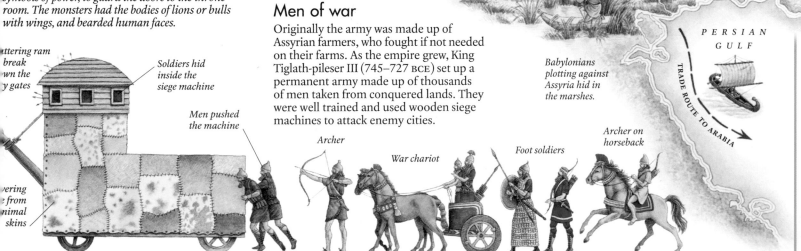

attering ram break wn the y gates

Soldiers hid inside the siege machine

Men pushed the machine

vering e from nimal skins

Archer

War chariot

Foot soldiers

Archer on horseback

Celts—Iron Age Heroes

THE ROMANS AND GREEKS called a series of people who lived beyond their frontiers Celta, Galli, and Keltoi, and wrote of them as barbarians who drank too much and indulged in nasty human sacrifices. But the Celts were actually highly skilled metalworkers who made sophisticated iron weapons, strong armor, and sturdy war chariots. They were also fearsome warriors who boasted of their conquests with songs and poems.

The Celtic culture, with its distinctive objects made of iron, bronze, and gold, probably developed around Hallstatt in modern-day Austria by about 750 BCE. Its second great phase, from about 500 BCE, is called La Tène. Celtic tribes spread across much of Europe, challenging opposition and settling in the areas they conquered. Their power was eventually threatened by Rome. By 54 BCE, Julius Caesar's ambitious plans and well-organized army had brought many Celtic lands under Roman rule.

This bronze and iron helmet, with gold leaf decoration, was found in an old channel of the Seine River, France.

Colorful characters

The Celts liked bright clothes, especially woolen cloaks, which were often patterned with checks and stripes. They also wore eye-catching jewelry, including bracelets on their arms and wrists and solid gold necklaces. This personal display was carried into battle. When armies met, men boasted of their deeds and those of their ancestors, daring opponents to fight them. Sometimes a war would be settled by two champions fighting each other.

SHETLAND ISLANDS

NORTH SEA

SCOTLAND

In Scotland, the Celts made small artificial islands, called crannogs, in lochs and rivers for houses.

IRELAND

The Celts crafted spectacular bronze trumpets.

WALES

ENGLAND

Maiden Castle

Desborough
Colchester

In 60 CE, Queen Boudicca and the Iceni tribe rose against the Romans, who had taken Britain into their empire.

The Veneti, a seagoing Celtic tribe, were defeated by Julius Caesar during his conquest of Gaul.

Celts threw prized objects into the streams and lakes that were sacred to their gods and goddesses.

This imported bronze vessel, or krater, was used for mixing wine. It was buried with a Celtic princess at Vix.

RHINE

Reinheim

Vix

SEINE

Alesia   **La Tène**

C E L T I C

LOIRE

G A U L

Julius Caesar took the heavily defended hill fort at Alesia during his conquest of Gaul.

Iron was made in special furnaces.

RHONE

Roquepertuse

ATLANTIC OCEAN

Ribadeo

This popular style of necklace, called a lunula, was usually made of silver or gold.

DOURO

EBRO

Numantia

I B E R I A

TAGUS

Alcácer do Sal   **Mérida**

The Celts were avid hunters. Wild boar was a favorite quarry.

CORSICA

This bronze wine flagon from the 4th century BCE is a fine example of Celtic craftsmanship. A duck and a pack of hounds decorate the lid.

SARDINIA

M E D I T

A F R I C A

Daily life

The people of Celtic Europe were organized into tribes of varying sizes, led by chieftains. Women had rights, while the sick and old were well cared for. Most people were farmers living in small villages, but just before the Romans arrived in Britain and Gaul, some Celts began to live in larger settlements that might be called towns. Houses were built of wood or stone, according to what was available locally. Roads were paved with wooden beams.

A scene inside a typical Celtic home

An enemy's skull was often placed over the door.

The frame was made of wooden posts with a roof of thatch, or straw.

Women cooked meals in an iron cauldron that hung on a long chain.

The walls were made of woven branches plastered with clay, known as wattle and daub.

Before battle, warriors in Britain painted blue patterns on their bodies.

Men often shaved their cheeks but kept a long moustache.

Children played a game with a ball and stick, like hockey.

The tribes the Romans called Germani lived east of the Rhine River.

GERMANY

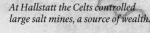

The Celts were efficient farmers. They used a special reaping machine to harvest the grain.

Magnificent bronze mirrors, such as this one found at Desborough, England, were status symbols.

Skulls and sacrifices

The Celts made sacrifices to their gods of valuable objects—and sometimes people too. Roman writers said the Celts believed their souls would go to the next world, rest awhile, and then be reborn on earth. They believed their souls were in their heads, and so saved the skulls of honored ancestors or great enemies. Religious leaders were known as druids.

Human skulls were displayed in stone shrines like these found at Roquepertuse in southern France.

Feasts and festivals

The Celts celebrated festivals with grand feasts, songs, and games. Wine was common, but the most popular drink was beer. The Celts loved music, and poet-musicians, called bards, learned long poems about heroes and their deeds. They sang them at their chieftain's feasts, accompanying themselves on harps. They also wrote songs that poked fun at their chief's enemies.

Forts and fights

To protect themselves, the Celts built hilltop fortresses and surrounded them with huge earth walls and wooden palisades (fences). Wars between tribes were common, so the hill forts offered safety to people and their treasure. Celtic warriors often fought as individual heroes. They did not even join forces to fight the disciplined units of the Roman army. Only in Ireland and northern Scotland did the Celts escape Roman conquest.

DANUBE

E U R O P E

llein (zburg) · Hallstatt

At Hallstatt the Celts controlled large salt mines, a source of wealth.

A chieftain and his family, dressed up for a festival.

TIBER

DANUBE

B L A C K S E A

Celts known as Galli migrated eastward, settling in an area of Asia Minor named Galatia.

Ancyra (Ankara)

G A L A T I A

A D R I A T I C S E A

Rome ·

ITALY

GREECE

Pergamum

A S I A M I N O R

The Celts invaded Rome in 387 BCE. One area was saved from attack when cackling geese raised the alarm.

SICILY

In 279 BCE, a group of migrating Celts invaded Greece and sacked the shrine of the god Apollo at Delphi.

Delphi

Many Gauls killed themselves and their families after being defeated by Attalos I of Pergamum in 240 BCE.

CYPRUS

| 0 | 100 | 200 | 300 Kilometers |

| 0 | 50 | 100 | 150 | 200 Miles |

M E D I T E R R A N E A N S E A

CRETE

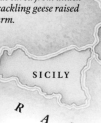

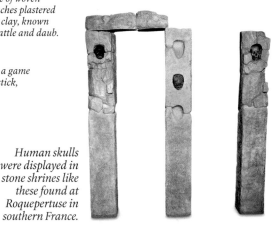

Persia—The Magnificent Empire

IN JUST 30 YEARS the Persians grew from being a minor tribe on the fringes of Babylon to ruling the world's most powerful nation. The Persians and their neighbors, the Medes, first moved into what is now Iran in about 1300 BCE and ruled the area for many years. In 559 BCE, Cyrus became king of the Persians and, 10 years later, took over the kingdom of Media, even though the king was his grandfather. He defeated the Greek colonies in Ionia, and conquered the kingdom of Lydia, rich in gold. In 539 BCE, he seized the mighty Babylonian Empire.

For more than 200 years the kings of Persia ruled supreme. The Persians were skilled warriors, horse riders, and craftworkers. They were also highly organized. To control the vast empire, which now stretched from Egypt to India, King Darius I (522–486 BCE) divided the land into provinces. Sturdy roads linked the farthest corners of the empire, and tributes and taxes poured into the palaces at Persepolis and Susa.

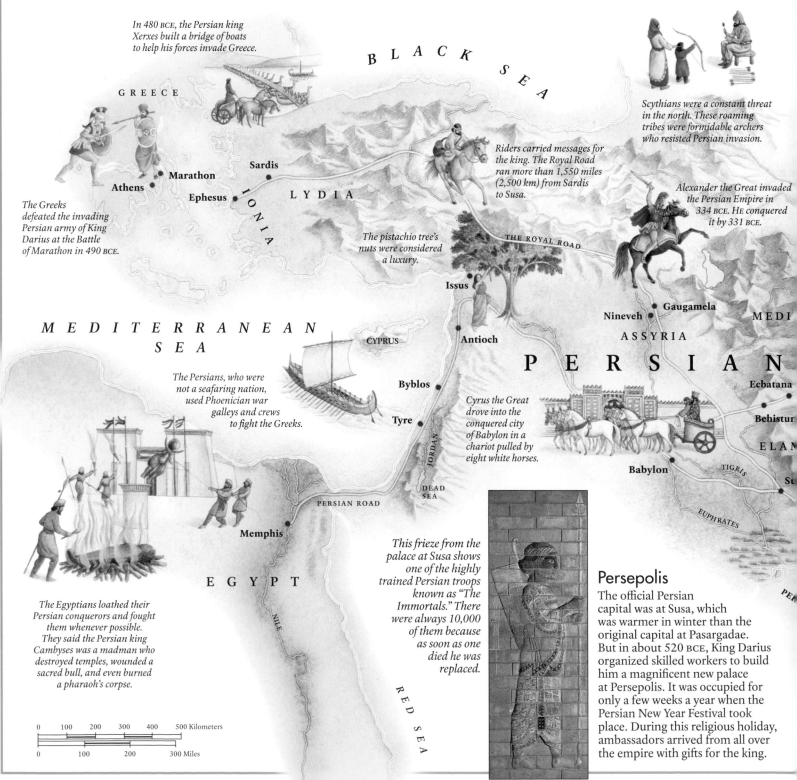

In 480 BCE, the Persian king Xerxes built a bridge of boats to help his forces invade Greece.

Scythians were a constant threat in the north. These roaming tribes were formidable archers who resisted Persian invasion.

Riders carried messages for the king. The Royal Road ran more than 1,550 miles (2,500 km) from Sardis to Susa.

Alexander the Great invaded the Persian Empire in 334 BCE. HE conquered it by 331 BCE.

The Greeks defeated the invading Persian army of King Darius at the Battle of Marathon in 490 BCE.

The pistachio tree's nuts were considered a luxury.

The Persians, who were not a seafaring nation, used Phoenician war galleys and crews to fight the Greeks.

Cyrus the Great drove into the conquered city of Babylon in a chariot pulled by eight white horses.

The Egyptians loathed their Persian conquerors and fought them whenever possible. They said the Persian king Cambyses was a madman who destroyed temples, wounded a sacred bull, and even burned a pharaoh's corpse.

This frieze from the palace at Susa shows one of the highly trained Persian troops known as "The Immortals." There were always 10,000 of them because as soon as one died he was replaced.

Persepolis

The official Persian capital was at Susa, which was warmer in winter than the original capital at Pasargadae. But in about 520 BCE, King Darius organized skilled workers to build him a magnificent new palace at Persepolis. It was occupied for only a few weeks a year when the Persian New Year Festival took place. During this religious holiday, ambassadors arrived from all over the empire with gifts for the king.

BLACK SEA
GREECE
Sardis
Athens Marathon
Ephesus
IONIA
LYDIA
MEDITERRANEAN SEA
CYPRUS
Issus
Antioch
Byblos
Tyre
JORDAN
DEAD SEA
PERSIAN ROAD
Memphis
EGYPT
NILE
RED SEA
THE ROYAL ROAD
Nineveh Gaugamela
MEDI
ASSYRIA
PERSIAN
Ecbatana
Behistur
ELAM
Babylon
TIGRIS
EUPHRATES
Su

0 100 200 300 400 500 Kilometers

0 100 200 300 Miles

The King of Kings

The Persian monarchs claimed the title "King of Kings" to show their total power over other rulers. The king had supreme power and everywhere he went he was surrounded by fawning courtiers and officials, chosen from the noblest families. He also had many wives who lived in a special household called a harem. But people were constantly plotting to murder the king. To avoid a sticky end, kings often had their male relatives killed, just in case they posed a threat.

This model of a Persian chariot is made of gold. It was part of the Oxus Treasure found near the Oxus River, in the province of Bactria (part of modern Afghanistan).

The King's Ears

The Persian Empire was so vast that it was divided into 20 provinces, called satrapies. Each satrapy was ruled by a governor, or satrap, acting on the king's behalf. Loyalty was important. The king needed to know if his officials were collecting the correct amount of tax or if they were taking more and pocketing the extra. And so special servants, known as "The King's Ears," listened for the slightest hint of treachery.

The Greek wars

There was no love lost between the Greeks and the Persians. When the Greek colonies in Ionia lost their independence to the Persians, the armies of mainland Greece came to their aid, sparking a series of Persian attacks. King Darius I and King Xerxes invaded Greece in 490 and 480 BCE, respectively. The outnumbered Greeks suffered several setbacks, but they defeated each invasion, with victories on land and sea. The wars left the Greeks with a hatred of Persians and a desire for revenge. They finally achieved this under Alexander the Great.

This mosaic shows the Persian King Darius III fleeing from Alexander during the Battle of Issus in 333 BCE.

The Massagetae were nomads who withstood Persian attempts to conquer them. King Cyrus died during a campaign against them.

This silver drinking vessel, or rhyton, was made around 400 BCE. The griffin at its base was an imaginary creature often used in Persian decoration.

Caravans of Bactrian camels carried silver, spices, and ivory across the empire.

This gold armlet is part of the Oxus Treasure.

BACTRIA

Bactra

PERSIAN ROAD

E M P I R E

Kabul

Taxila

Alexandria Areion
(Herat)

The palace at Persepolis had high-columned audience halls, store rooms for tributes, and army barracks.

The satrap of an Indian province watched his staff weigh gold to be taken to the king of Persia.

INDIA

So speaks Zarathustra

Originally the Persians worshipped many deities. Then, some time between 1200 and 600 BCE, a prophet called Zarathustra (also called Zoroaster) preached of a supreme god of goodness, light, and truth named Ahura Mazda, the Wise Lord. But there were also evil, darkness, and lies in the world. People had to choose which to follow and after death they would be rewarded or punished according to the life they had led. Fire played an important part in the Zoroastrian religion, and was thought to represent the truth of the Wise Lord.

Pasargadae

polis

Priests looked after the altar bearing the sacred fire of Zoroastrianism, a religion still practiced today.

The King of Kings received tribute from all parts of his empire. This scene was carved along the stone stairway leading to the main audience hall at Persepolis.

Assyrian bringing a pony

Indian carrying pots of gold dust

Babylonian leading a prize bull

Elamite offering a young lion

Greece—The Power and the Glory

By about 800 BCE, a glorious new culture had begun to emerge on the Greek mainland, bringing fine art and great buildings. The Greeks studied music and wrote plays, puzzled over mathematics and medicine, and discussed political ideas. They introduced a system of government in which men had a say in how their city state was run.

But Greece was not a united country. The hot, often mountainous mainland and islands were divided into many small city-states, each with its own farmlands and villages. The most powerful city-state was Athens, which became the center of Greek civilization and culture in the 5th century BCE. It had a well-trained army and the most powerful navy in the ancient world.

Power to the people

Each of the city states in Greece was called a *polis*, from which we get the English word "politics." By about 510 BCE, most had gotten rid of their kings, preferring to be ruled by a small group of leaders (an oligarchy) or by one powerful politician (a tyrant). In 508 BCE, Athens introduced the idea of democracy, meaning "rule by the people." This gave ordinary men a chance to help make decisions. Male citizens decided on the law by voting at a meeting called the Assembly. Women, foreigners, and enslaved people were not allowed to vote.

The Athenians chose the powerful politician Pericles to lead them from 443 to 429 BCE. He organized building the Acropolis temples.

The Greek colonies

The population of the city states grew so rapidly that, between 750 and 550 BCE, many Greeks were forced overseas. They spread around the Black Sea and to those parts of the Mediterranean where their rivals, the Phoenicians, had not already set up colonies. Once settled, they farmed and built cities in the Greek style, introducing their own way of life and culture. They also set up trading links with their homeland.

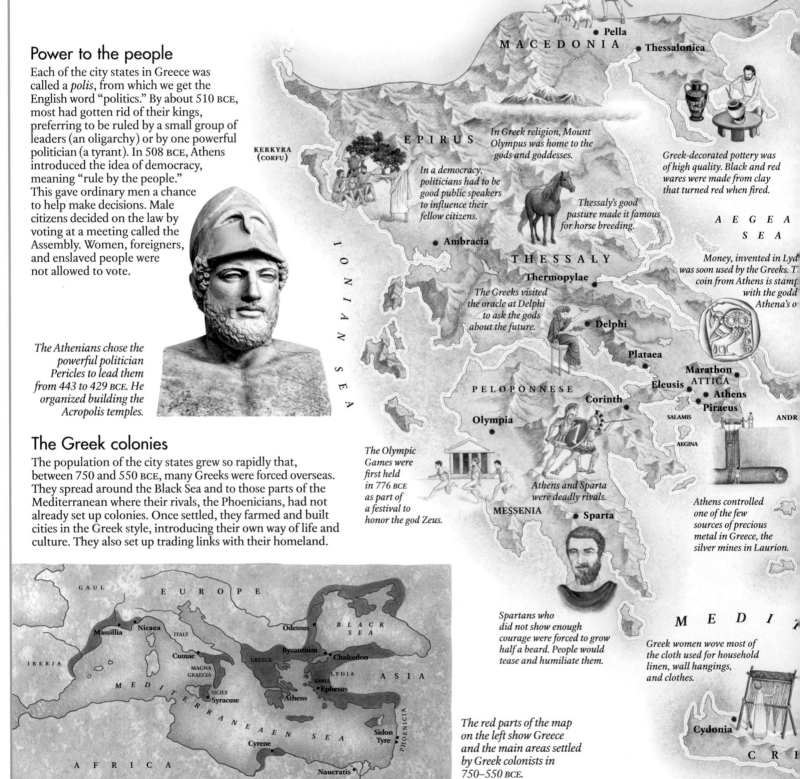

A Macedonian shepherd. The Greeks saw the Macedonians as not true Greeks.

MACEDONIA
Pella
Thessalonica

KERKYRA (CORFU)

EPIRUS

In Greek religion, Mount Olympus was home to the gods and goddesses.

Greek-decorated pottery was of high quality. Black and red wares were made from clay that turned red when fired.

In a democracy, politicians had to be good public speakers to influence their fellow citizens.

Thessaly's good pasture made it famous for horse breeding.

AEGEAN SEA

Ambracia

THESSALY

Money, invented in Lyd was soon used by the Greeks. T coin from Athens is stamp with the godd Athena's o

Thermopylae

The Greeks visited the oracle at Delphi to ask the gods about the future.

Delphi

Plataea

Marathon

PELOPONNESE

Eleusis
ATTICA

Corinth

Athens

Olympia

SALAMIS
Piraeus

AEGINA

ANDR

The Olympic Games were first held in 776 BCE as part of a festival to honor the god Zeus.

Athens and Sparta were deadly rivals.

MESSENIA

Sparta

Athens controlled one of the few sources of precious metal in Greece, the silver mines in Laurion.

Spartans who did not show enough courage were forced to grow half a beard. People would tease and humiliate them.

MEDITE

Greek women wove most of the cloth used for household linen, wall hangings, and clothes.

GAUL

EUROPE

Massilia
Nicaea
ITALY

Odessus

BLACK SEA

Byzantium

IBERIA

GREECE
Chalcedon

MAGNA GRAECIA

LYDIA

SICILY
Syracuse

IONIA
Ephesus

ASIA

MEDITERRANEAN SEA

Athens

PHOENICIA

Sidon
Tyre

Cyrene

AFRICA

Naucratis

EGYPT

The red parts of the map on the left show Greece and the main areas settled by Greek colonists in 750–550 BCE.

Cydonia

CR

This painting shows the fierce battle of Salamis, key to repelling invasion by the Persian king Xerxes. Under their leader, Themistocles, the Athenians had built a battle fleet. They lured the Persians into the narrow channel between the island of Salamis and the mainland and defeated them.

The Persian wars

The Persians invaded Greece in 490 BCE and 480 BCE. The Greeks suffered the plunder of Athens and the massacre of a small Spartan army guarding the narrow pass of Thermopylae. Despite these losses, the Greeks eventually won with land victories at Marathon and Plataea and a naval victory at Salamis. At sea, the Greeks' main weapon was a ship called a trireme, designed to ram enemy ships and hole them below the waterline. The ships fought battles by breaking through lines of enemy boats, turning, ramming, and then retreating.

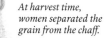

At harvest time, women separated the grain from the chaff.

Byzantium

THRACE

In 480 BCE, the Persians marched their army into Greece.

Troy

LEMNOS

One of the most famous Greek poets was Sappho, a woman from the island of Lesbos.

LESBOS

A Spartan way of life

The city-state of Sparta controlled the southern part of Greece, the Peloponnese. After the Spartans conquered Messenia, they dedicated themselves to war, seeking to quell rebellions and repel invasions. All true Spartans had to be warriors, and training, which started at the age of seven, was tough. Boys were whipped to prepare them for battle. Girls were raised to be fit and strong so that they would give birth to healthy Spartan babies. Their military skill helped Sparta win the Peloponnesian Wars fought against Athens in 431–404 BCE.

CHIOS

Women wore dresses in the Ionic (left) or Doric (right) styles.

The city of Athens

Athens became the largest and most prosperous city-state in Greece. It controlled the silver mines in the south and had excellent trading links from its port at Piraeus. Standing above Athens was the rocky hill called the Acropolis, which means "high city." It was sacred, with beautiful temples and shrines to the goddess Athena. Athens had splendid buildings, paved streets, and an open market and general meeting place called the *agora*. Scholars such as Socrates, Plato, and Aristotle taught there.

This bronze figure shows a tough Spartan warrior. Spartan soldiers wore helmets, breastplates, and leg coverings called greaves to protect themselves.

The great altar stood at the side of Athena's temple, instead of in front, as was usual.

The Parthenon was dedicated to the goddess Athena. It was built from marble in 447–438 BCE.

Ephesus

Herodotus, the "father of history," was the first to try to record events accurately.

The Acropolis in Athens

SAMOS
Miletus

A colored frieze showed the battle of the centaurs, half man, half horse Greek mythical figures.

NAXOS

Halicarnassus

This temple, the Erechtheum, contained an ancient wooden statue of Athena.

(TORINI)

Food shortages forced some islanders to leave Thera for North Africa. When they gave up and headed home, they weren't allowed to land.

RHODES

A bronze statue of the goddess Athena the Defender stood 30 ft (9 m) tall.

Religious processions wound their way through Athens, entering the sacred enclosure on the Acropolis through a gateway called the Propylaea.

The temple of Athena Nike, the goddess in her role as bringer of victory.

Most Greek warships were triremes, with three levels of oarsmen on each side.

0	25	50	75	100 Kilometers

0	25	50	75 Miles

RRANEAN SEA

Greece–Alexander and After

ALEXANDER THE GREAT was one of the finest generals the world had ever known. His campaigns were brilliantly planned. By 323 BCE, he had conquered an empire that stretched from Greece to Asia Minor and all the way to India. His career of conquest lasted 11 years and covered more than 20,000 miles (32,000 km).

Alexander was born in 356 BCE in the kingdom of Macedonia, once an enemy of Athens. After the murder of his father, King Philip II, the 20-year-old Alexander became king. He inherited a large, experienced army of Greeks and Macedonians, and completed his father's plan to finish off the hated Persians.

Alexander left men behind in the lands he conquered. It helped spread the Greek language and culture over an enormous area, and resulted in some of the world's most impressive building styles and important ideas being absorbed into later civilizations. He died of a fever, when only 33 years old, while preparing to invade Arabia.

Alexander the Great

Alexander traveled huge distances to extend his empire, founding cities along the way, all named Alexandria. He had little time to run his empire but tried to get Greeks and his new subjects to be friendly. But when Alexander died, his generals murdered his wife Roxane and his young son, then fought each other for control of the empire. Antigonus took Greece, Ptolemy got Egypt, and Seleucus held the Middle East.

Alexander on his favorite horse, Bucephalus.

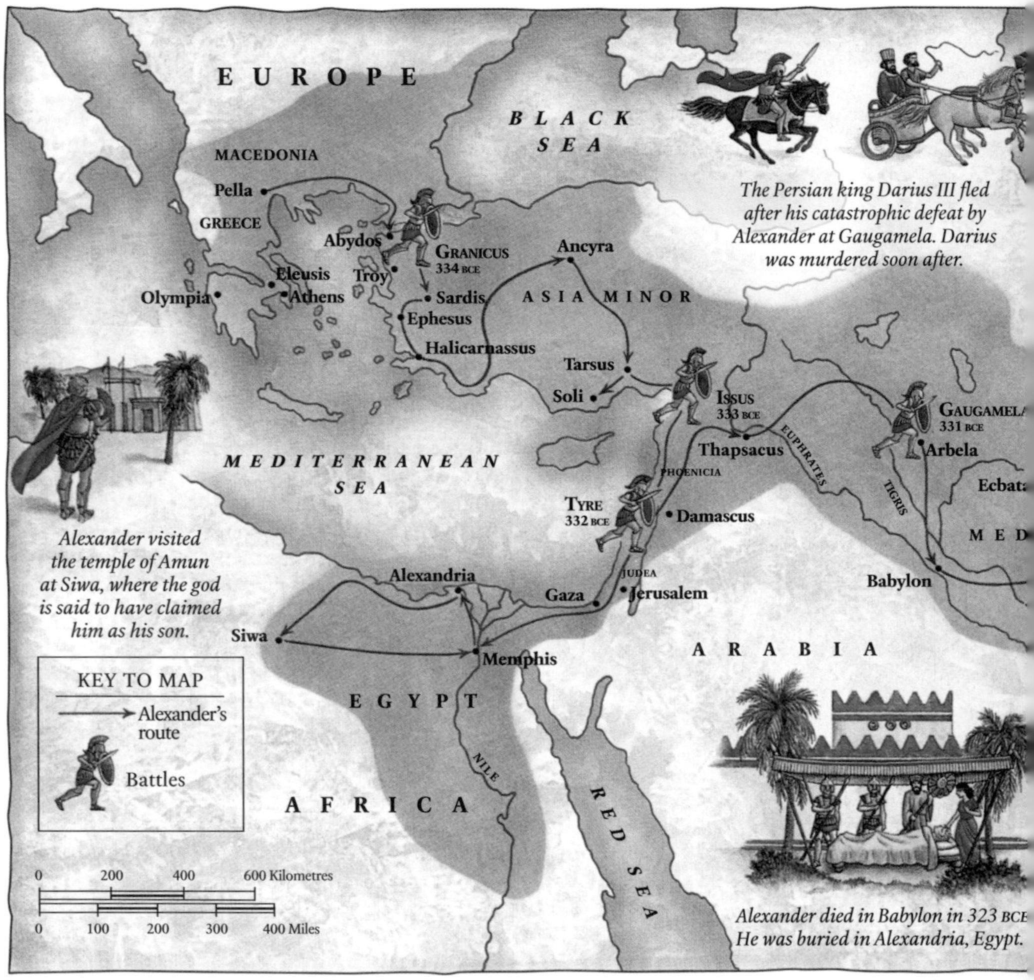

Alexander on the move
This map shows the main events in Alexander's life. While taking the kingdoms of Asia Minor, Alexander won two great battles against the Persians at Granicus and Issus. He turned south, taking Phoenicia, Judea, and Egypt. He then beat the Persians at Gaugamela, before going to India, where he was victorious at the Hydaspes River.

The Persian king Darius III fled after his catastrophic defeat by Alexander at Gaugamela. Darius was murdered soon after.

Alexander visited the temple of Amun at Siwa, where the god is said to have claimed him as his son.

KEY TO MAP
→ Alexander's route
🏃 Battles

0   200   400   600 Kilometres
0 100 200 300 400 Miles

Alexander died in Babylon in 323 BCE. He was buried in Alexandria, Egypt.

Map labels: EUROPE, BLACK SEA, MACEDONIA, Pella, GREECE, Abydos, GRANICUS 334 BCE, Ancyra, Eleusis, Troy, Sardis, Ephesus, ASIA MINOR, Olympia, Athens, Halicarnassus, Tarsus, Soli, ISSUS 333 BCE, GAUGAMELA 331 BCE, Arbela, MEDITERRANEAN SEA, EUPHRATES, Thapsacus, PHOENICIA, Ecbata, TIGRIS, TYRE 332 BCE, Damascus, MED, Alexandria, JUDEA, Gaza, Jerusalem, Babylon, Siwa, Memphis, ARABIA, EGYPT, AFRICA, NILE, RED SEA

Gods and goddesses

The Greeks had 12 major deities, five of them shown here. The others were Hera, goddess of women and wife of Zeus, and her sister Hestia, guardian of the hearth and home. Apollo was god of the sun and music and twin brother of Artemis. Aphrodite was goddess of love and beauty while Hades was god of the Underworld. Ares (son of Zeus and Hera) was god of war and Hermes was the messenger of the gods. Less important gods cared for different aspects of life and death.

Artemis, the huntress, was goddess of the moon, and protector of women and children.

Zeus, king of the gods, controlled thunder. The eagle was his symbol.

Demeter, goddess of the grain, had the power to make wheat, barley, and all living things grow.

Poseidon, god of the sea, holds a trident, symbol of the fisherman.

Athena, daughter of Zeus, was goddess of wisdom and war, and the patroness of Athens.

A thirst for knowledge

In the 6th century BCE, Greek scholars began trying to find out all they could about life and the universe. Such men were called philosophers, meaning "lovers of knowledge." They asked questions about how the body worked, calculated mathematical problems, studied animals, and watched the movement of the planets. These early Greek studies formed the basis of modern biology, medicine, mathematics, astronomy, and philosophy.

Pythagoras was born on the Greek island of Samos in about 560 BCE. An astronomer and mathematician, he is remembered for his theorem on triangles.

Reliefs and statues decorated the exterior, most painted in red and blue.

Columns surrounded the temple. A main room housed the statue of a god or goddess.

The Greeks built impressive temples for their gods. These Doric temple remains stand in southern Italy.

Greek temples were built on stepped platforms.

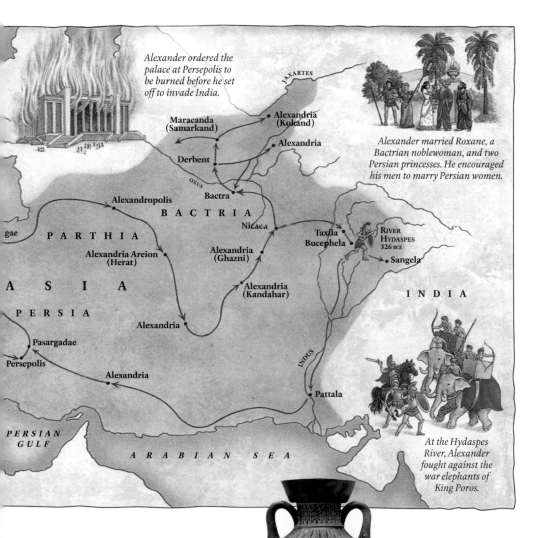

Alexander ordered the palace at Persepolis to be burned before he set off to invade India.

JAXARTES

Maracanda (Samarkand)

Alexandria (Kokand)

Alexandria

Derbent

OXUS

Alexandropolis

Bactra

B A C T R I A

gae

P A R T H I A

Nicaea

Taxila
Bucephela

RIVER
HYDASPES
326 BCE

A S I A

Alexandria Areion
(Herat)

Alexandria
(Ghazni)

Sangela

P E R S I A

Alexandria
(Kandahar)

I N D I A

Pasargadae

Alexandria

Persepolis

Alexandria

INDUS

Pattala

P E R S I A N
G U L F

A R A B I A N   S E A

Alexander married Roxane, a Bactrian noblewoman, and two Persian princesses. He encouraged his men to marry Persian women.

At the Hydaspes River, Alexander fought against the war elephants of King Poros.

Built to last

Most homes in Greece were simple brick and wood buildings with earth floors. The Greeks lavished money and skill on public buildings, especially the temples. Although originally made of wood and thatch, from the 6th century BCE, temples were made from stone or marble with roofs of baked clay tiles. The architects took care to achieve a look of balance and harmony and many buildings were decorated with columns. There were two main styles—Doric, a simple style with sturdy, plain columns; and Ionic, more elegant with thinner, decorated columns. Many public buildings were also adorned with friezes, statues, and wall paintings.

The Greek theatre at Miletus in modern-day Turkey is still used for plays.

The Olympic Games

Athletics contests were held as part of all important religious festivals in Greece. The most important were the Olympic Games, which were held every four years and lasted five days. As it was the duty of every male citizen to fight for his city-state in wartime, he had to keep himself fit. Many events at the games, such as throwing the javelin, wrestling, and boxing, were based on military skills. During the games, all wars stopped so that contestants could travel in safety to Olympia from all over the empire.

This Greek clay vase is decorated with figures in a chariot race, an Olympic Games event. Women were not allowed to take part in, or even watch, the games.

Drama

The first great plays were written by the Greeks. As part of the Dionysia, a festival in Athens to honor the god Dionysus, poets composed and performed songs. These gradually got longer, with more performers taking part, until they had grown into plays. Only men could perform and all actors wore masks. There were three types of plays—comedies, tragedies, and satyrs, which poked fun at serious topics. Plays were performed in open-air theatres and prizes were awarded for the best new play in each category.

Rome—From Villages to Empire

THE ROMAN EMPIRE was the strongest force the western world had ever seen. By 117 CE, under the rule of the emperors, Rome controlled most of Europe, North Africa, and a large part of the Middle East. But the story of the Romans began in about 750 BCE with a group of farmers who lived on the hills overlooking the Tiber River. Gradually their villages merged into one powerful city. Before long, the tough peasants, who made excellent soldiers, began to dominate the people around them. By 264 BCE, they had control of Italy.

Over the years the Romans trained armies to conquer new territories, and built a network of roads. They introduced their Latin language, their style of building, and their system of government to the conquered areas. When the western part of the empire collapsed in 476 CE, many things were left behind that still influence our life today.

Octavian, Rome's first emperor, was given the title Augustus ("the revered one").

Rulers of Rome

At first Rome was ruled by kings. Then in about 507 BCE the Romans set up a republic—a government run by nobles elected by the citizens. This lasted for nearly 500 years. But by 49 BCE Rome was plunged into civil war. To restore peace, in 27 BCE the Romans gave power to one man—Octavian—who became the first Roman emperor. Some later emperors ruled well, but others were cruel, or mad. Domitian murdered anyone who disagreed with him. Caligula made his horse a senator.

Julius Caesar, a Roman general, was assassinated by rivals on March 15, 44 BCE.

In about 122 CE the emperor Hadrian ordered the building of a stone wall to defend the northern frontier.

BRITAIN

Londinium (London)

SILCHESTER

Julius Caesar conquered Gaul in 51 BCE and twice invaded Britain in 55–54 BCE.

G A U L

Hannibal, a Carthaginian general, attacked Rome in 218 BCE. He marched 40,000 men and 37 elephants across the Alps.

Ships stayed in port from November to March to avoid winter storms.

Burdigala (Bordeaux)

NIME

Massilia (Marseille)

ATLANTIC OCEAN

Roman engineers built this aqueduct in Segovia to bring in water from the nearby hills.

Tarraco (Tarragona)

Supplies of grain and olive oil were shipped to the port of Ostia, just south of Rome.

H I S P A N I A

ITALICA

Gades (Cadiz)

Carthago Nova (Cartagena)

M E D I T E

A F R I C A

ROMAN ROAD

This map shows how the Roman Empire changed, reaching its greatest extent in about 220 CE.

300 BCE
100 BCE
220 CE

BRITAIN
GERMANY
GAUL
Rome
ITALY
HISPANIA
ANATOLIA
SYRIA
MEDITERRANEAN SEA
AFRICA
EGYPT

The Senate

During the Republic, Rome was governed by two officials (consuls) assisted by the Senate, a group of men (senators) who passed the laws. At first, the senators all came from the rich (patrician) families of Rome. Both the consuls and senators were voted into office each year by ordinary citizens (plebeians). Later, after strikes and demonstrations, the plebeians were given the power to stop laws from being passed. However, the emperors took this power away.

A senator wore a white toga edged with a purple stripe.

0   100   200   300   400 Kilometers

0   100   200   300 Miles

Road builders

The Romans built a huge network of roads. These helped the army move quickly into battle, provided a route for a postal system, and made trade easier. The roads ran straight, using bridges or viaducts (arches) to cross rivers or valleys. Roman roads were so well built that they survived for hundreds of years. Many modern European roads still follow the routes they took.

A permanent fort for the Roman army

Horse stables

Headquarters

High defensive wall

The barracks housed up to 80 soldiers in each block.

Border patrols quelled local uprisings.

Augusta Treverorum (Trier)

The emperor Marcus Aurelius defended his empire against invasion on the frontier along the Danube River.

The Roman army

The Romans were able to rule their empire and conquer others because of their army. They had the best-trained, best-equipped army in the world. Roman armies, divided into groups called legions, fought in formation using swords and spears. Each night they built a temporary camp, dismantling it in the morning. Permanent forts were built on the empire's frontiers.

Every legion carried a standard that identified the unit. The eagle was the symbol of Jupiter, king of the Roman gods.

Bigger and better buildings

Initially, the Romans copied many Greek building styles. But in the 2nd century BCE, they found a way to make concrete out of volcanic ash, allowing bigger and stronger builds. They developed the arch, which took the weight of a building and let them span greater distances than before. Arches were used to build bridges, aqueducts, and amphitheatres such as Rome's Colosseum, where gladiator fights were popular.

Every Roman city had an open space—the forum. Some of Rome's forum buildings still stand today.

Religion

The Romans worshipped many gods and goddesses who looked after various aspects of their life. Then a new religion—Christianity—became popular. Its followers believed that Jesus Christ was the son of the one God of the Jews. Although Jesus was put to death, Christianity spread rapidly, and in 391 CE it became the official faith of the empire.

GERMANY

DANUBE

CARNUNTUM

ALPS

Aquileia

Barbarians, the name for foreign invaders, finally overran the Roman Empire. The most famous were led by Attila the Hun.

Viminacium

DANUBE

ROMAN ROAD

Durostorum (Silistra)

BLACK SEA

TIBER

ADRIATIC SEA

Rome

THE COLOSSEUM

ITALY

RSICA

Marble was quarried in Greece for the fine buildings in Rome.

Byzantium (Istanbul)

Trapezus (Trabzon)

ROMAN ROAD

ARDINIA

ANATOLIA

Wild animals were brought from India and Africa to fight in arenas across the empire.

IONIAN SEA

GREECE

AEGEAN SEA

Ephesus

TRADE ROUTE FROM CHINA

SICILY

Rhegium (Reggio di Calabria)

Syracuse

arthage

Antioch

CYPRUS

SYRIA

R

EL DJEM

R
R
A
N
E
A
N

S
E
A

CRETE

Trade ships took grain and linen from Egypt to Rome.

Rome and Carthage battled at sea for control of Sicily during the first Punic War (264–241 BCE).

Leptis Magna

JUDEA

Jerusalem

A raised center allowed rainwater to run into ditches at the sides.

The road was paved with thick stone slabs.

Workers, often enslaved people, dug a trench and filled it with layers of stones and gravel.

Cleopatra of Egypt married Mark Antony, a Roman general. They killed themselves after defeat by Octavian at the Battle of Actium (31 BCE).

Alexandria

NILE

TRADE ROUTE FROM INDIA

EGYPT

RED SEA

Jesus Christ was crucified in the Roman province of Judea during the reign of the emperor Tiberius.

Rome—Life in the City

ABOUT ONE MILLION PEOPLE were crowded into the city of Rome by the year 300 CE. It was a magnificent city, with palaces for the emperor and his family, beautiful houses for the very rich, and triumphal arches and columns. There were several forums—open spaces used as markets and for social and political gatherings—as well as theatres, libraries, public baths, and shops selling goods from all over the empire. Life for the rich was very pleasant. The poor people did not do as well. They lived in overcrowded apartment blocks in areas that were dirty, noisy, smelly, and often downright dangerous. These buildings were badly built with so many floors that they often collapsed or caught fire, killing the people inside. Life was even worse for the thousands of enslaved people who were brought back to Rome as the empire grew. They had to do all the dirty, heavy work or train to fight—and probably die—as gladiators in the Colosseum.

The official garment of a Roman citizen was the toga. *It was made from a large piece of semicircular white woolen cloth, worn over a tunic.*

The Romans loved to celebrate. This painting by Sir Lawrence Alma-Tadema (1836–1912) shows a procession for the festival of Ceriales, held every April to honor Ceres, the goddess of grain.

Family life

The father was the head of his family, and held the power of life and death over them. A new baby had to be accepted into the family by its father or it would be left outside to die. Once accepted, a baby was a good reason for a party, and the house was decorated with leaves and flower garlands. After nine days, a baby boy was given a protective charm called a *bulla* to wear around his neck. When children grew older, their parents decided whom they would marry.

The tunic was usually worn on its own by poorer people who found it more comfortable for work.

Girls and boys wore tunics. When a boy turned 14, he went to the forum where he took off his childhood charm and put on the toga *of an adult male citizen.*

A woman wore a fine wool tunic. Over this went a stola, *a robe that reached to her feet. A garment called a* palla *could be draped over the* stola.

A scene inside a Roman house

Tiles were made from a clay mold, then baked until hard.

Houses and shops

Only the very rich could afford their own house, or *domus*. Most Romans lived in an apartment block (*insula*). The ground floor of an *insula* was taken up by small shops open to the street. The higher up you went, the smaller and cheaper the rooms. Few rooms had cooking facilities, so tenants bought hot food from local shops. Cheap rooms had no running water, but there were public lavatories and drinking fountains in each street.

Going to school

Rich parents sent their sons to school or educated them at home with private tutors, who were often Greek. Boys went to school when they were about six. They learned reading, writing, and math. When they were 11, they went to a more advanced teacher, the *grammaticus*, to study literature, history, math, and astronomy. By the age of 14, those who wanted to be politicians went on to study rhetoric (public speaking). Girls learned household skills at home. Poorer children had to work.

First-floor apartments had large rooms with comfortable furniture.

Shops sold bread, meat, vegetables, fruit, and household items.

Dogs scavenged the streets for scraps.

Streets were often dirty, with graffiti scrawled on the walls.

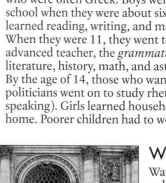

The Trevi Fountain was built in about 1750 CE to use water from an ancient Roman aqueduct, the Aqua Virgo.

Waterworks

Water was needed to supply public baths, lavatories, and drinking fountains. The baths were huge buildings with hot and cold pools where thousands went for a bath, a massage, and to gossip. Water was brought into Rome by aqueducts, structures with channels to carry the water. The rich had water piped directly to their homes, paying for it according to the size of the pipes used. Many tried to avoid paying by secretly joining their pipes to the main network.

CITY WALL

Map of Rome

This map shows the layout of Rome in about 300 CE. Temples, triumphal arches, forums, bath houses, grand tombs called mausoleums, and aqueducts were set up by different emperors and named after them. The wall to defend the city was built by the emperor Aurelian in 270 CE.

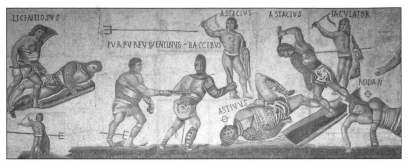

This mosaic shows gladiators trying to kill each other. Gladiators were criminals or enslaved people trained to fight for entertainment.

Home decorating

The Romans admired Greek art and used Greek sculptors and artists to decorate their buildings and homes. City houses were often plain on the outside, but rich Romans painted the inner walls with scenes from mythology, gardens, or the countryside. Elegant statues of gods and goddesses were placed around the house. Floors were covered with mosaics – pictures and patterns made from small pieces of colored stone. A wealthy home would also have elegant furniture of wood, bronze, and marble and perhaps a display of antique Greek vases.

This painting shows what a battlefield the Colosseum could be. The Romans adored the idea of exotic animals. Lions, tigers, leopards, rhinoceroses, and bears were brought from all over the world to fight for the crowds.

The Roman games

The Romans loved to be entertained. The most popular events were chariot races, gladiator fights, or wild beast hunts. The games attracted huge, enthusiastic crowds who placed money on who would win the races or fights. The bloodthirsty crowds watched wild beasts fight each other to the death. Gladiators also fought each other using swords, nets, and spears in their struggle to survive. Gladiators were named after the sword, or *gladius*, that they carried. If a gladiator was wounded, the crowd decided whether he would live or die by giving a "thumbs up" or "thumbs down" sign.

KEY TO MAP

1 Mausoleum of Hadrian	9 Forum of Trajan
2 Mausoleum of Augustus	10 Roman Forum
3 Gardens of Lucullus	11 Tiber Island
4 Arch of Claudius	12 Colosseum
5 Stadium of Domitian	13 Trajan Baths
6 Pantheon of Hadrian	14 Temple of Claudius
7 Baths of Diocletian	15 Circus Maximus
8 Camp of the Praetorian Guard	16 Baths of Caracalla

The Riches of Arabia

THE DESERTS OF ARABIA are among the world's hottest and driest places. The people who lived in these hostile lands belonged to nomadic tribes who moved from one water hole to another, depending on the vegetation that grew briefly after the light winter rains. Along the fertile coasts of the west and south, however, there were busy trading cities with paved roads and settled peoples. In the city of Mecca, the religion of Islam was born.

In the southern kingdoms, the Arabs enjoyed fabulous riches. They built a spectacular dam at Marib to control the water supply for their agriculture. But it was trade that made the Arabs rich. Resin from frankincense and myrrh trees provided neighboring civilizations with incense for their religious ceremonies. Merchants traded in gold, gems, and ivory, as well as copper, tin, and iron, and wide-ranging trade networks reached not only the Mediterranean world but also East Africa, India, and China.

TRADE ROUTE TO ROME

Palmyra

Tyre

MEDITERRANEAN SEA

Alexandria

NABATAEA

Petra

SINAI

EGYPT

Tay

Nabataean craftsmen made finely decorated pots.

Berenice

RED SEA

Life in the desert

The name given to the nomadic Arab people was *bedouin*, meaning "desert dweller." Each family lived in a large tent that provided shade from the sun but was warm in the cold desert nights. Bedouin people grazed sheep and goats and later raised horses and camels. The camel made an enormous difference when it was domesticated in about 1100 BCE. Camels can travel up to 100 miles (160 km) a day for eight days without water in extreme heat. People could now cross the deserts.

Arabs used camels very effectively in battle. This stone carving from Assyria shows how Arab rulers fought off Assyrian invasions.

Temples, tombs, and monuments were cut into rock in the city of Petra, in modern-day Jordan. This building is the Ad Deir (*The Monastery*).

The Nabataeans

The Nabataeans were an Arab tribe who lived in Arabia's north. In the 4th century BCE, they founded a kingdom that covered the earlier biblical land of Edom. Their capital city was Petra, which controlled the overland route for incense from southern Arabia. They also had the only reliable source of water in the area, which they brought into the city through a series of channels and pipes. At the height of their power, in the 1st century CE, the Nabataeans controlled areas as far north as Damascus, but the Romans took over their kingdom in 106 CE.

A new faith emerges

The Prophet Mohammed was a camel caravan leader whose deep religious faith had major consequences. The early Arabs had worshipped several deities, but Mohammed preached that there was only one God, Allah. At first, his message was not well received by the people of his home town, Mecca. He fled to Medina but returned in 630 CE with a victorious army. After this, the new faith, Islam, spread rapidly. Followers, called Muslims, have five religious duties: to believe in one God and acknowledge Mohammed as His Prophet; to pray five times a day, facing Mecca; to give charity; to fast during the month of Ramadan; and to visit Mecca at least once.

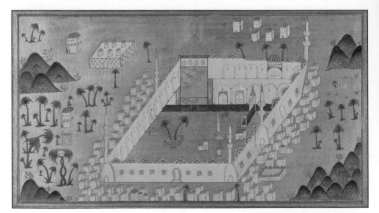

This tile painting shows the Holy Mosque of the Prophet Mohammed, which was built in Medina. The mosque houses Mohammed's tomb, making Medina one of Islam's holiest cities.

The map on the right shows the growth of the Islamic Empire between 632 CE, when Mohammed died, and 750 CE, when the expansion ended.

632 CE
750 CE

The spread of Islam

Inspired by their new faith of Islam, the Arabs surged out of Arabia. They rapidly captured a vast empire that stretched across the Middle East to India, and across North Africa into southern Europe. As they went, they converted most inhabitants to Islam. They also absorbed much from the culture and learning of their new provinces, creating a glorious new civilization of their own.

Queen Zenobia ruled the city of Palmyra and united many Arab provinces against their Roman masters. She was eventually captured by the emperor Aurelian and taken to Rome.

Arab chiefs used saluki dogs to hunt. Lions (now extinct in the area) were the greatest prize.

Bedouin people lived in tents made from woven goat hair. Camels were essential to their survival, but horses were their passion.

Arab ships, called dhows, traded with India and Africa.

Thousands of warriors rode into the defeated city of Mecca on the first pilgrimage.

Merchants traveled overland by camel in groups called caravans.

The Kaaba ("Cube") at the center of the Grand Mosque in Mecca, Islam's holiest city.

The bark of frankincense and myrrh trees was cut to release resin, which was used as incense.

Marib's 7th century BCE dam broke in the 6th century CE, causing terrible damage.

This modern photo taken in Yemen, in the southwest corner of Arabia, shows fertile terraced fields cut into the land.

Harvesting apricots

It is thought that multistory mud-brick houses existed in the 3rd and 4th centuries BCE.

Fortunate Arabia

Along the fertile coasts of Arabia, there was enough water to grow grain, fruits, and vegetables. Arabia interested the Romans, who knew only of the fertile areas and the wealth gained from the incense trade. They called the country "Fortunate Arabia." The emperor Augustus sent an expedition into the interior in 25 BCE, but, hearing of a land of scorching sand, he abandoned all ideas of conquest.

In 570 CE, the people of Aksum invaded and marched toward Mecca. A smallpox epidemic is said to have forced their withdrawal.

0   100   200   300 Kilometers
0 50 100 1500 200 Miles

Africa—Kingdoms of Gold

AFRICA IS A VAST CONTINENT where the first humans are thought to have evolved. From about 700 CE great kingdoms rose and fell, isolated from the rest of the world by the huge Sahara Desert. More than 3,000 years ago, Africa south of the Sahara was inhabited by tribal peoples who lived by hunting and gathering. Gradually, however, Bantu-speaking people migrated out of the forests of West Africa and made their way east and south. They reached the area around the Congo River by about 500 BCE, and southern Africa by about 400 CE. Some of the first major African cities emerged in the Bantu heartland of West Africa. Kingdoms such as Ghana, Mali, Songhay, and Benin traded gold with Muslims who had invaded North Africa in the 8th century CE. Over to the east was Meroë, Africa's first great civilization outside of Egypt. To the south, the impressive stone fortress kingdom of Great Zimbabwe was built, a major religious, political, and trading center.

These Nubian pyramids at Meroë were built as tombs for kings, queens, and wealthy citizens.

Kingdom of Meroë

To the south of Egypt lay the lands of Nubia and Kush. Their peoples were dominated by Egypt, but in 728 BCE, they seized power and ruled Egypt for almost 100 years. Eventually they withdrew south and, in the 3rd century BCE, set up a capital at Meroë. They built an impressive royal residence of brick and stone, a temple for Apedemak, their lion god, and steep-sided pyramid tombs. Their art, architecture, and religion were influenced by Egypt, but evolved a unique style. They were also among the earliest people to develop an alphabet. They raised cattle, grew cotton, and used oxen to drive waterwheels. The population included skilled ironworkers, and merchants who traded with the Mediterranean world and India. Meroë was overrun in the 4th century CE by people from Aksum.

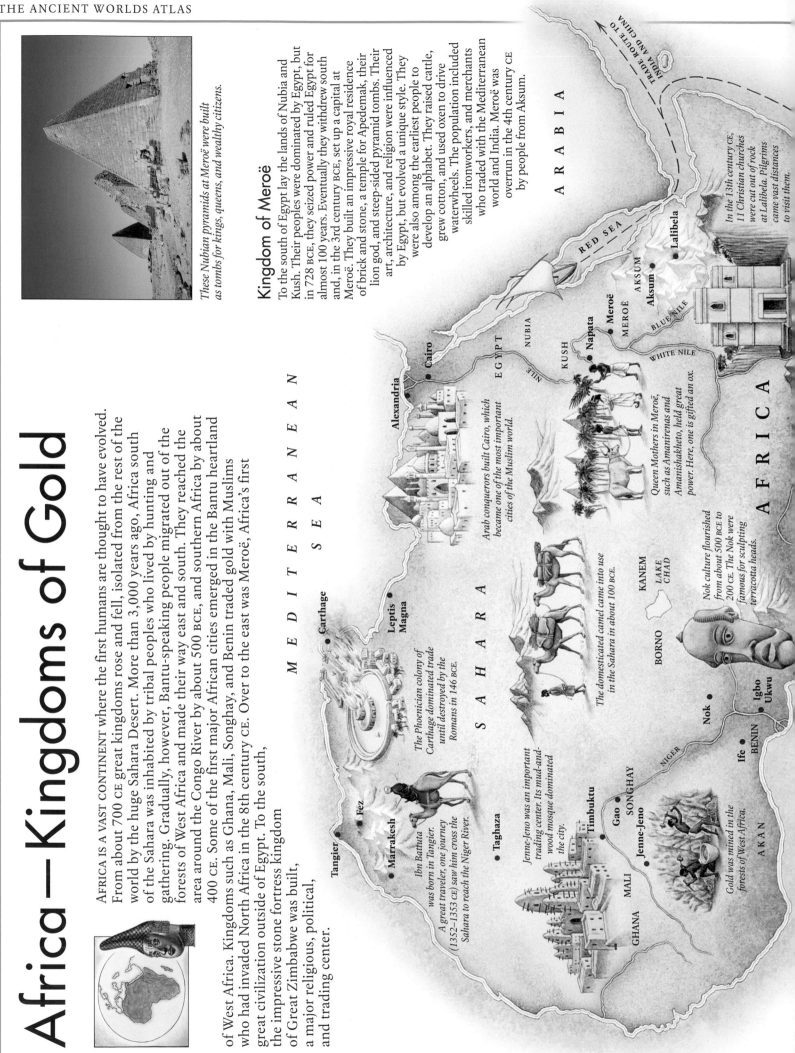

The Phoenician colony of Carthage dominated trade until destroyed by the Romans in 146 BCE.

Ibn Battuta was born in Tangier. A great traveler, one journey (1352–1353 CE) saw him cross the Sahara to reach the Niger River.

Jenne-Jeno was an important trading center. Its mud-and-wood mosque dominated the city.

Gold was mined in the forests of West Africa.

The domesticated camel came into use in the Sahara in about 100 BCE.

Nok culture flourished from about 500 BCE to 200 CE. The Nok were famous for sculpting terracotta heads.

Arab conquerors built Cairo, which became one of the most important cities of the Muslim world.

Queen Mothers in Meroë, such as Amanirenas and Amanishakheto, held great power. Here, one is gifted an ox.

In the 13th century CE, 11 Christian churches were cut out of rock at Lalibela. Pilgrims came vast distances to visit them.

MEDITERRANEAN SEA

TRADE ROUTE TO INDIA AND CHINA

RED SEA

ARABIA

AFRICA

SAHARA

NILE

BLUE NILE

WHITE NILE

EGYPT

NUBIA

KUSH

Carthage

Leptis Magna

Tangier

Fez

Marrakesh

Taghaza

Timbuktu

Gao

Jenne-Jeno

SONGHAY

MALI

GHANA

Nok

AKAN

BENIN

Ife

Igbo Ukwu

BORNO

KANEM

LAKE CHAD

NIGER

Alexandria

Cairo

Napata

Meroë

MEROË

Aksum

AKSUM

Lalibela

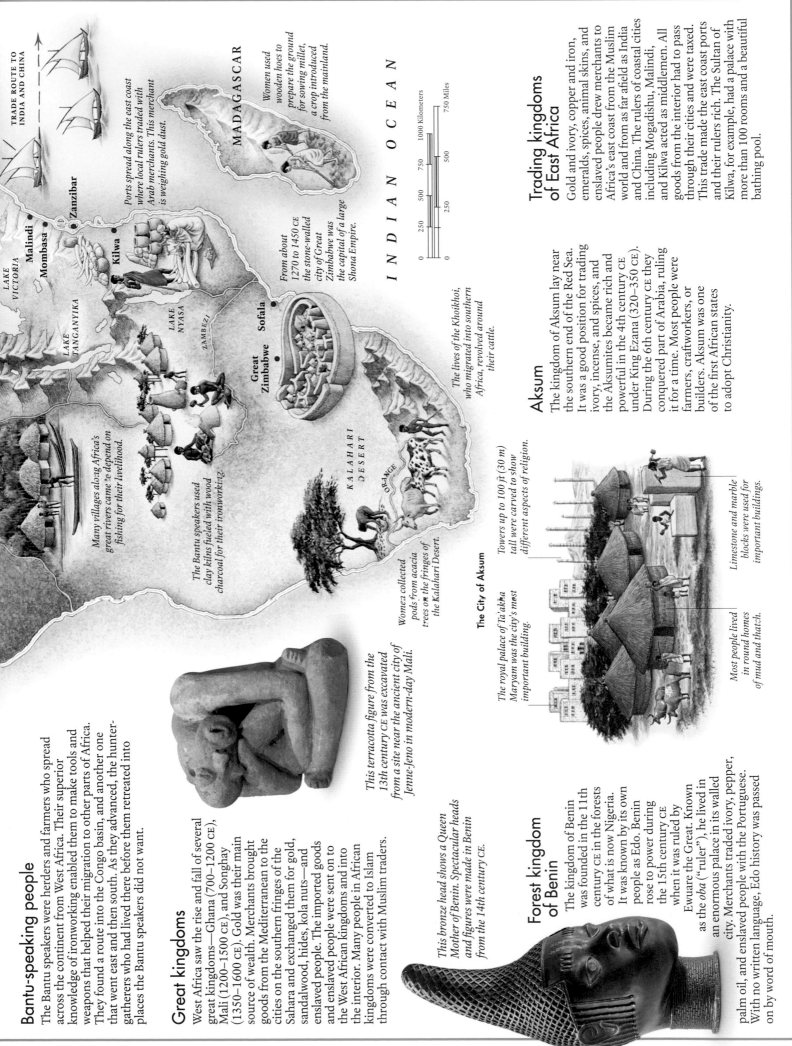

Bantu-speaking people

The Bantu speakers were herders and farmers who spread across the continent from West Africa. Their superior knowledge of ironworking enabled them to make tools and weapons that helped their migration to other parts of Africa. They found a route into the Congo basin, and another one that went east and then south. As they advanced, the hunter-gatherers who had lived there before them retreated into places the Bantu speakers did not want.

Great kingdoms

West Africa saw the rise and fall of several great kingdoms—Ghana (700–1200 CE), Mali (1200–1500 CE), and Songhay (1350–1600 CE). Gold was their main source of wealth. Merchants brought goods from the Mediterranean to the cities on the southern fringes of the Sahara and exchanged them for gold, sandalwood, hides, kola nuts—and enslaved people. The imported goods and enslaved people were sent on to the West African kingdoms and into the interior. Many people in African kingdoms were converted to Islam through contact with Muslim traders.

This terracotta figure from the 13th century CE was excavated from a site near the ancient city of Jenne-Jeno in modern-day Mali.

Forest kingdom of Benin

The kingdom of Benin was founded in the 11th century CE in the forests of what is now Nigeria. It was known by its own people as Edo. Benin rose to power during the 15th century CE when it was ruled by Ewuare the Great. Known as the *oba* ("ruler"), he lived in an enormous palace in its walled city. Merchants traded ivory, pepper, palm oil, and enslaved people with the Portuguese. With no written language, Edo history was passed on by word of mouth.

This bronze head shows a Queen Mother of Benin. Spectacular heads and figures were made in Benin from the 14th century CE.

TRADE ROUTE TO INDIA AND CHINA

Ports spread along the east coast where local rulers traded with Arab merchants. This merchant is weighing gold dust.

Women used wooden hoes to prepare the ground for sowing millet, a crop introduced from the mainland.

MADAGASCAR

ZANZIBAR
Malindi
Mombasa
Kilwa

LAKE VICTORIA
LAKE TANGANYIKA
LAKE NYASA
ZAMBEZI

Sofala
Great Zimbabwe

From about 1270 to 1450 CE the stone-walled city of Great Zimbabwe was the capital of a large Shona Empire.

Many villages along Africa's great rivers came to depend on fishing for their livelihood.

The Bantu speakers used clay kilns fueled with wood charcoal for their ironworking.

KALAHARI DESERT
ORANGE

Women collected pods from acacia trees on the fringes of the Kalahari Desert.

The lives of the Khoikhoi, who migrated into southern Africa, revolved around their cattle.

INDIAN OCEAN

1000 Kilometers
750 Miles

0   250   500   750
0   250   500

Aksum

The kingdom of Aksum lay near the southern end of the Red Sea. It was a good position for trading ivory, incense, and spices, and the Aksumites became rich and powerful in the 4th century CE under King Ezana (320–350 CE). During the 6th century CE they conquered part of Arabia, ruling it for a time. Most people were farmers, craftworkers, or builders. Aksum was one of the first African states to adopt Christianity.

Trading kingdoms of East Africa

Gold and ivory, copper and iron, emeralds, spices, animal skins, and enslaved people drew merchants to Africa's east coast from the Muslim world and from as far afield as India and China. The rulers of coastal cities including Mogadishu, Malindi, and Kilwa acted as middlemen. All goods from the interior had to pass through their cities and were taxed. This trade made the east coast ports and their rulers rich. The Sultan of Kilwa, for example, had a palace with more than 100 rooms and a beautiful bathing pool.

Towers up to 100 ft (30 m) tall were carved to show different aspects of religion.

The royal palace of Ta'akha Maryam was the city's most important building.

Limestone and marble blocks were used for important buildings.

Most people lived in round homes of mud and thatch.

The City of Aksum

India—The Mauryan Age

A DYNASTY OF KINGS called the Mauryans ruled India in 322–185 BCE. They came to power hundreds of years after the collapse of the Indus Valley civilization. By about 600 BCE, the Aryan invaders of the Indus Valley had merged with the rest of the Indian population. They introduced their Sanskrit language and composed sacred hymns, called the Vedas, that laid the foundation of their society and Hindu religion. But the country was still divided into small kingdoms that constantly challenged each other for overall power.

A bigger threat came from the west. In 327 BCE, Alexander the Great, who had recently defeated the Persians, marched his army into India. But his exhausted troops soon headed home. It was at this point that a young Indian warrior, Chandragupta Maurya, seized power. First, he overthrew the ruling kingdom of Magadha. Then he challenged the Greek general Seleucus, who had taken over part of Alexander's empire. Chandragupta proved a clever ruler and a great soldier, who established the Gupta dynasty. By the time his grandson Asoka took over, India was already united into its first great empire.

Chandragupta drove out the remaining Greeks and became ruler of the land Alexander had occupied.

Asoka sent envoys to Egypt and Libya, requesting they take up his Buddhist hopes for an end to war.

TO EGYPT

INDUS

Harvesting mangoes

A R A B I A N   S E A

Asoka the convert

The Mauryan Empire reached its peak under Asoka's rule. He came to power in about 272 BCE with a violent reputation for war. The turning point in his life came after the Battle of Kalinga, which saw more than 100,000 soldiers and civilians killed. Asoka was so horrified that he converted to Buddhism. He began to practice the Buddha's laws of nonviolence and encouraged peace. He arranged for hospitals to be built, and introduced plans to protect the forests. After his death, the Mauryan Empire went into decline. In 185 BCE, it was overthrown by the Shunga Empire.

No pictures of Mauryan kings remain, but this wall painting shows the rich style of later Indian rulers.

The pillar at Sarnath was the first of many monuments erected by Asoka. It was topped by four lions seated over four wheels of the law, symbols of Buddhism. The lions were adopted as the crest of modern India.

Buddha—the enlightened one

Siddhartha Gautama was born in 563 BCE into a princely Indian family. When he left home he saw so much suffering that he decided to take time away to meditate on the meaning of life. In the India of his time, people believed they were reborn many times, paying in each life for the mistakes (or being rewarded for the goodness) of the life before. After six years of study and prayer, Gautama achieved enlightenment (complete understanding) and was called the Buddha, or "enlightened one."

Buddha taught followers how to achieve nirvana *and escape the endless cycle of rebirth.*

Building works

In embracing Buddhism, Asoka built and encouraged others to build monasteries and sacred mounds called stupas. He also erected sandstone pillars across the empire, each engraved with pledges to rule with kindness and truth. Craftsmen from Persia contributed to the style of the stone work. The Mauryan rulers lived in a palace at Pataliputra. As there was not enough good local stone for building, the palace was made of wood from the tropical forests. It was set in a park with gardens, lakes, and even a race track.

The Stupa of Sanchi was built during Asoka's reign. Stupas were mound-shaped monuments built over sacred relics at places connected with the Buddha's life.

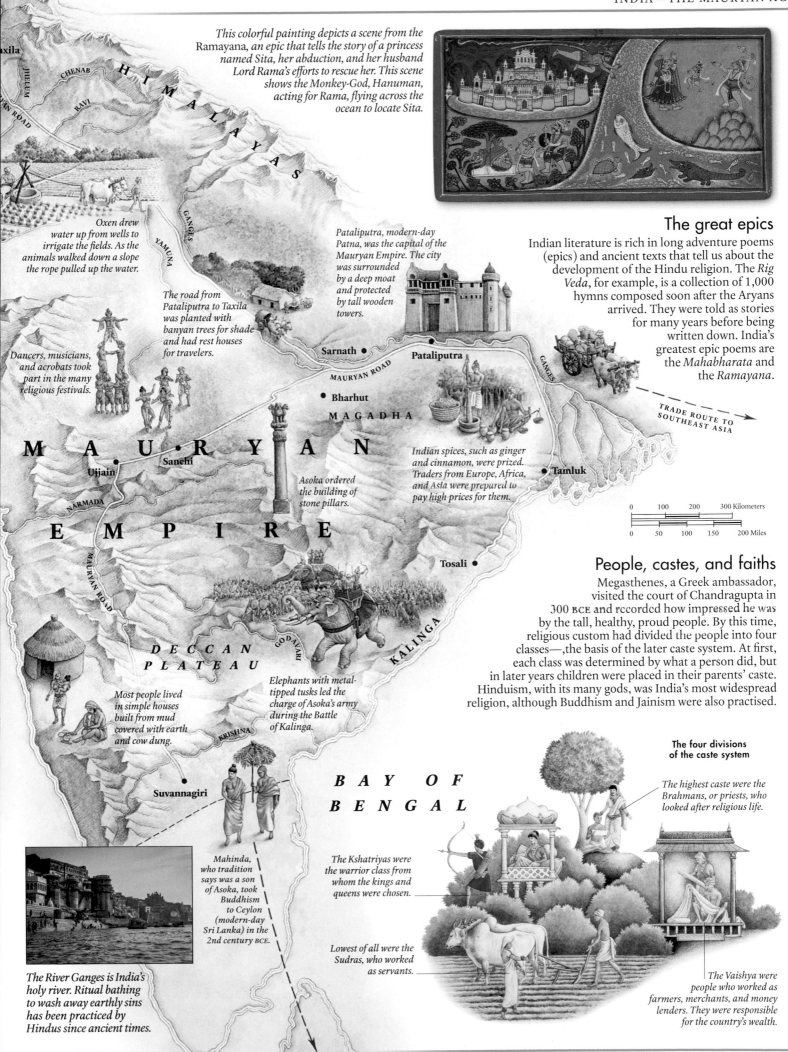

This colorful painting depicts a scene from the Ramayana, an epic that tells the story of a princess named Sita, her abduction, and her husband Lord Rama's efforts to rescue her. This scene shows the Monkey-God, Hanuman, acting for Rama, flying across the ocean to locate Sita.

The great epics

Indian literature is rich in long adventure poems (epics) and ancient texts that tell us about the development of the Hindu religion. The *Rig Veda*, for example, is a collection of 1,000 hymns composed soon after the Aryans arrived. They were told as stories for many years before being written down. India's greatest epic poems are the *Mahabharata* and the *Ramayana*.

Oxen drew water up from wells to irrigate the fields. As the animals walked down a slope the rope pulled up the water.

Pataliputra, modern-day Patna, was the capital of the Mauryan Empire. The city was surrounded by a deep moat and protected by tall wooden towers.

The road from Pataliputra to Taxila was planted with banyan trees for shade and had rest houses for travelers.

Dancers, musicians, and acrobats took part in the many religious festivals.

Sarnath

Pataliputra

MAURYAN ROAD

Bharhut

MAGADHA

Indian spices, such as ginger and cinnamon, were prized. Traders from Europe, Africa, and Asia were prepared to pay high prices for them.

Tamluk

TRADE ROUTE TO SOUTHEAST ASIA

Ujjain

Sanchi

Asoka ordered the building of stone pillars.

Tosali

People, castes, and faiths

Megasthenes, a Greek ambassador, visited the court of Chandragupta in 300 BCE and recorded how impressed he was by the tall, healthy, proud people. By this time, religious custom had divided the people into four classes—,the basis of the later caste system. At first, each class was determined by what a person did, but in later years children were placed in their parents' caste. Hinduism, with its many gods, was India's most widespread religion, although Buddhism and Jainism were also practised.

DECCAN PLATEAU

KALINGA

Most people lived in simple houses built from mud covered with earth and cow dung.

Elephants with metal-tipped tusks led the charge of Asoka's army during the Battle of Kalinga.

Suvannagiri

B A Y   O F   B E N G A L

The four divisions of the caste system

The highest caste were the Brahmans, or priests, who looked after religious life.

Mahinda, who tradition says was a son of Asoka, took Buddhism to Ceylon (modern-day Sri Lanka) in the 2nd century BCE.

The Kshatriyas were the warrior class from whom the kings and queens were chosen.

Lowest of all were the Sudras, who worked as servants.

The River Ganges is India's holy river. Ritual bathing to wash away earthly sins has been practiced by Hindus since ancient times.

The Vaishya were people who worked as farmers, merchants, and money lenders. They were responsible for the country's wealth.

CEYLON

47

China—The First Emperor

UNTIL THE YEAR 221 BCE, China was divided into separate states, each with its own king. These rival kingdoms had been at war for more than 250 years. Then Zheng, king of the state of Qin (pronounced "Chin," from which we get the name China), emerged as the victor. To show his superior power, he gave himself the grand title Qin Shi Huangdi ("First Qin Sovereign Emperor").

Zheng vowed to keep the country together. He removed the old rulers, forcing them to live in the capital at Xianyang, and divided the country into new districts with officials to see that everything was run efficiently. Zheng ordered the building of a road and canal network and sent a vast task force of workers to build the Great Wall of China. But despite all Zheng's efforts, the empire collapsed soon after his death in 210 BCE.

The First Emperor ordered the burning of books that disagreed with his ideas.

The Tiger of Qin

Zheng came to the throne of Qin at just 13 years old. He was a brilliant general and politician with a tough character that earned him the nickname the "Tiger of Qin." However, he was afraid of death. His grand palace had more than 1,000 bedrooms and he spent each night in a different room in case he was killed while he slept. In the end, he died of natural causes.

Setting standards

The First Emperor needed to unite the land and rebuild its wealth after the years of war. To make this easier, things were standardized. The many characters of the written language were made the same all over the land. Lots of goods had to bear the maker's name; if items were faulty, the maker could be punished. Cart axles had to be the same width so the wheels used ruts long worn into the roads.

Weights and measures had to be the same. This jade weight is from the province of Qin.

The Great Wall

China had long been in danger from the nomadic Xiongnu tribes (the Huns) in the north. Local rulers had tried to keep them out by building a series of walls. In 214 BCE, the First Emperor ordered these to be joined into one huge wall more than 2,150 miles (3,460 km) long. Thousands of peasants were sent to work on this wall. The weather was often wet and cold, and conditions were dangerous. Men who died were buried where they fell.

Crossbow bolts were shot through windows.

The wall was 30 ft (9 m) tall and wide enough for a chariot.

Watchtowers were built along the wall.

Stone slabs covered an earth and rubble interior.

Soldiers guarded against attack.

Peasants were forced to work on the wall.

An overseer held a whip.

Scaffolding was made from bamboo poles.

Workers moved earth using simple tools, such as spades and picks, baskets, and wheelbarrows.

The palace at the imperial capital

Blast furnaces were used to make cast iron, producing stronger weapons and better farm tools.

General Meng Tian was responsible for building the wall. He sent officials to inspect the work.

GOBI DESERT

THE GREAT WALL

YELLOW RIVER

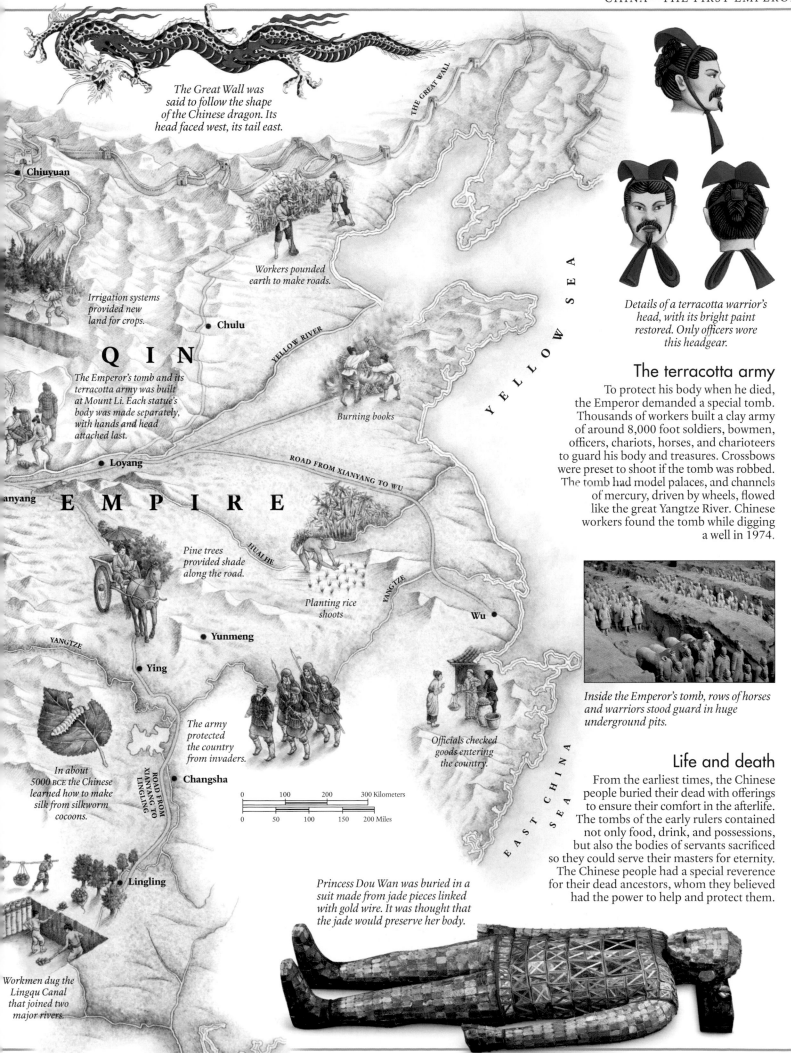

The Great Wall was said to follow the shape of the Chinese dragon. Its head faced west, its tail east.

THE GREAT WALL

Chiuyuan

Workers pounded earth to make roads.

Irrigation systems provided new land for crops.

Q I N

Chulu

YELLOW RIVER

The Emperor's tomb and its terracotta army was built at Mount Li. Each statue's body was made separately, with hands and head attached last.

Burning books

Loyang

ROAD FROM XIANYANG TO WU

anyang

E M P I R E

Pine trees provided shade along the road.

HUAI HE

Planting rice shoots

Y
E
L
L
O
W

S
E
A

Details of a terracotta warrior's head, with its bright paint restored. Only officers wore this headgear.

The terracotta army

To protect his body when he died, the Emperor demanded a special tomb. Thousands of workers built a clay army of around 8,000 foot soldiers, bowmen, officers, chariots, horses, and charioteers to guard his body and treasures. Crossbows were preset to shoot if the tomb was robbed. The tomb had model palaces, and channels of mercury, driven by wheels, flowed like the great Yangtze River. Chinese workers found the tomb while digging a well in 1974.

YANGTZE

Yunmeng

Ying

In about 5000 BCE the Chinese learned how to make silk from silkworm cocoons.

Wu

Officials checked goods entering the country.

The army protected the country from invaders.

ROAD FROM XIANYANG TO LINGLING

Changsha

0   100   200   300 Kilometers

0   50   100   150   200 Miles

Inside the Emperor's tomb, rows of horses and warriors stood guard in huge underground pits.

Life and death

From the earliest times, the Chinese people buried their dead with offerings to ensure their comfort in the afterlife. The tombs of the early rulers contained not only food, drink, and possessions, but also the bodies of servants sacrificed so they could serve their masters for eternity. The Chinese people had a special reverence for their dead ancestors, whom they believed had the power to help and protect them.

Lingling

Workmen dug the Lingqu Canal that joined two major rivers.

Princess Dou Wan was buried in a suit made from jade pieces linked with gold wire. It was thought that the jade would preserve her body.

E
A
S
T

C
H
I
N
A

S
E
A

North American Peoples

THE EARLIEST SETTLERS in North America arrived from Asia at least 20,000 years ago. At that time, the continents of Asia and America were joined by a bridge of land that disappeared under the sea at the end of the last Ice Age. Groups of hunters wandered across the land, following the animals on which they depended.

In this way, the hunter-gatherers spread out to populate North and South America—a vast area of widely varying temperatures and landscapes. Indigenous peoples of America—who were mistakenly named Indians by early explorers—learned to live in mountains and plains, forests and deserts, marshes, and frozen wastelands. Many were content to remain as hunter-gatherers, but some became farmers. Others settled in villages or large towns.

Hunters of the north

In the bitter cold of the far north, the Inuit adapted to the frozen land and sea. They hunted all the Arctic animals, birds, and fish, but their main supplies of food and clothing came from seals and caribou. In the winter, they traveled in search of food and lived in temporary homes made from blocks of hard-packed snow, called igloos. The Inuit also built cabins of stone, turf, and timber, or lived in tents.

The Makah people of Ozette harpooned whales from huge dugout canoes. One whale would supply the whole village with meat, oil, and bones for tools.

Indigenous nations of the Plains

The lands of the Plains nations (who had ancient names such as Blackfoot, Crow, and Dakota) stretched from the Rocky Mountains to the Mississippi valley, but most people lived on the fringes of the Plains and along the Missouri River. They planted crops in spring, gathered wild fruits in summer, and harvested in the autumn. Once or twice a year they hunted bison.

Many tribes lived in teepees, tents made from bison hide.

The mound builders

In about 200 BCE, a people we call the Hopewell began to replace the Adena in the Ohio River valley. They are known as mound builders because they buried their dead under earth mounds up to 40 ft (12 m) high. The Hopewell were traders who brought goods from as far away as the Rocky Mountains, the Great Lakes, the Gulf of Mexico, and the far north. They were also talented craftworkers who made fine pottery. For reasons that are unclear, the culture had disappeared by 550 CE.

BERING STRAIT

Walakpa

ALASKA

YUKON

Brooks River

MACKENZIE

GREAT BEAR LAKE

In summer, northern hunters lived in tents of caribou hide. Women prepared the caribou skin. Men decorated antlers using a bow drill.

Fishermen hunted the rivers, especially at rapids, and caught salmon with long spears.

Hunters dressed in caribou skins to camouflage them as they approached the herd.

N O
A M E

R O C K Y

Ozette

PACIFIC OCEAN

SNAKE

GREAT SALT LAKE

M T S

Acorns were shelled, dried, and pounded into flour. This was soaked to remove the tannic acid before use.

Mesa Verde

Pueblo Bonito

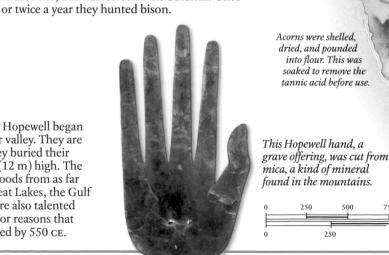

This Hopewell hand, a grave offering, was cut from mica, a kind of mineral found in the mountains.

Snaketown

Pueblo peoples dug irrigation systems to water crops of maize, beans, and squash.

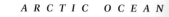

| 0 | 250 | 500 | 750 Kilometers |

| 0 | 250 | 500 Miles |

MEX

In winter, hunters of the north lived in igloos—round, domed houses built from blocks of snow laid in a spiral.

Thule

GREENLAND

BAFFIN ISLAND

Godthåb
Julianehåb

The Inuit hunted walrus from a kayak, or canoe, made of seal skin stretched over a wooden frame.

HUDSON BAY

...ribou came ...uth for the ... winter.

In about 1000 CE Leif Ericsson, from the Viking colony on Greenland, became the first European to set foot in America.

L'Anse aux Meadows

...RTH ...RICA

The Ojibwa people's domed houses were covered with bark or reed mats. Canoes were made of bark stretched over a wooden frame.

Wild rice grew around the Great Lakes. It was gathered in late summer by women in canoes.

LAKE SUPERIOR

LAKE MICHIGAN

LAKE HURON

ST LAWRENCE

LAKE ONTARIO

THE GREAT LAKES

LAKE ERIE

OHIO

In the northeastern woodlands, Iroquois women tended crops of maize, beans, and squash. The men hunted deer and birds, including wild turkeys. Houses were made of poles and elm bark.

MISSOURI

Cahokia

The Serpent Mound was built by the Hopewell people. It is 400 m (1,330 ft) from head to tail.

GREAT PLAINS

Spiro

People in Etowah ground pigment to make body paint.

Etowah

MISSISSIPPI

ATLANTIC OCEAN

People followed bison across the Plains using a carrying frame (called a travois) pulled by a domesticated dog.

Moundville

Hopewell people traded alligator teeth that they found in the swamps of Florida.

...O GRANDE

GULF OF MEXICO

Horses died out in North America in prehistoric times. When the Spanish arrived in Central America in the 1500s, they brought horses. Some escaped and they spread north.

This 19th century headdress was worn by the Sacred Women in the Blackfoot Sun Dance.

The Mississippians

The Mississippian culture, named after the great river at its center, emerged in about 700 CE. The Mississippians were maize-growing farmers but they also built large towns, such as Cahokia, Etowah, and Spiro. A feature of these towns was the flat-topped, rectangular earth mounds that provided platforms for temples made of timber and thatch. Houses for the rulers and nobles were built on top of smaller mounds. Their greatest town was Cahokia, which, at the height of its prosperity, housed about 10,000 people.

This pottery bottle from the Cahokia area of a mother nursing her child was probably made in about 1200 CE.

People of the Southwest

Two important cultures, the Hohokam and Ancestral Puebloan, developed in the dry conditions of the Southwest. The Hohokam, whose main village was Snaketown, built ball courts and platform mounds, and wove cotton cloth. They were clearly influenced by the civilizations of Mexico. In about 750 CE, the Ancestral Puebloans began building houses from sundried mud (adobe) bricks. Many of the villages, called *pueblos*, had large underground chambers (*kivas*) used for religious purposes.

Some pueblos, *such as the one in Mesa Verde, were built into a cliff.*

Spirits and medicine

Indigenous Americans believed that forceful beings (spirits) were present in all natural things. Farmers, for example,

were interested in the spirits that made their crops grow, while hunters needed guidance from the spirits that guarded wild animals. To help people deal with the spirit world, medicine men and women could contact the spirits, cure sickness, and foretell the future. These men and women wore elaborate headdresses with horns, fur, or feathers and their bodies may have been painted with sacred symbols. They may have also worn otter skin bags that held charms, medicinal herbs, and body paints.

The First Australians

THE FIRST AUSTRALIANS were nomadic people who arrived from Southeast Asia about 50,000 years ago across land which is now submerged. They originally settled around the fertile coasts and rivers but later moved across the continent, adapting to areas of rainforest, mountains, and desert. In desert areas, people lived in small groups, often moving camp in search of food. In more fertile areas, they built homes that could be used for several months.

First Australians still perform dances to reenact their ancestral past.

These original inhabitants were later called "Aboriginal people," meaning people who had lived there since the earliest times. They walked everywhere, each group traveling along familiar paths within its own territory. Many of these routes were thought to be the paths of their Dreamtime ancestors.

People in Arnhem Land built huts on platforms. Fires kept mosquitoes away and dogs called dingoes guarded the camp.

Along the northeast coast, people hunted turtles from outrigger canoes.

ARNHEM LAND

INDIAN OCEAN

Dancers painted their bodies with white, red, or yellow circles and lines. Music was played on a didgeridoo.

Tjukurpa stories were often told with earth drawings. Most designs were hidden from strangers. The design here was for an open ceremony.

CORAL SEA

An emu was lured into a trap by a man playing a wooden horn.

AUSTRALIA

Hunters caught kangaroos with boomerangs or spears.

Uluru, also known as Ayers Rock, has always been a sacred place for First Australians.

Men caught fish in the Murray and Darling rivers. They also caught waterfowl, shellfish, and platypus.

Women used stones to grind grass seeds. Wells were dug for drinking water.

DARLING

LACHLAN

MURRAY

Women used digging sticks to find yams, an edible root.

SOUTHERN OCEAN

MURRAY

Women beat fibers from tree bark to spin into string and weave into dilly bags.

People dug channels so that eels would swim inland to be caught and eaten.

Creator ancestors

The First Australians lived by a system of belief and law known as *Tjukurpa*. It was laid down when the ancestors traveled across the land, created its features, and gave it laws and morals. *Tjukurpa* continues today, as knowledge is passed down to each generation through stories, songs, dance, and art, teaching people how to behave and how to treat the land well.

The journeys of the ancestors were depicted in cave paintings.

The good earth

First Australians did not cultivate the land. Most of their time was spent finding food. Women searched for edible roots, grass seeds, grubs, and small animals. Men hunted larger animals such as kangaroos and possums, or caught fish and ducks from the rivers and coasts. People knew which trees to climb to find honey and birds' eggs. Trees also provided berries and nuts, as well as wood for boats, spears, and shields, and branches for shelter.

TASMAN SEA

TASMANIA

On Tasmania, women collected seashells to trade for items they needed.

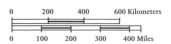

| 0 | 200 | 400 | 600 Kilometers |
| 0 | 100 | 200 | 300 | 400 Miles |

Polynesia and New Zealand

STEERING BY THE SUN AND STARS, the Polynesians settled most of the islands in the vast Pacific Ocean. To cross the great expanses of open sea, these skilled seafarers studied wind and wave patterns, interpreted cloud formations, and watched the behavior of certain land-based birds. Historians think that people originally set out from the islands of Southeast Asia about 4,000 years ago. Tonga and Samoa were settled first, then the Marquesas Islands and Tahiti. From there some sailors explored northward, reaching Hawaii by about 100 CE. Others headed east to Pitcairn, and still more reached Easter Island by about 400 CE. Although the way of life varied slightly from one group of islands to another, most early Polynesians lived in small communities grouped into tribes ruled by powerful chiefs. The last great journey, in about 950 CE, was undertaken by a group of Polynesians to a land they called Aotearoa—now New Zealand.

Sails made from palm-leaf matting

Coconut palm provided fiber for rope

Sheltered area for food supplies

Hull made from dugout tree trunk

HAWAIIAN ISLANDS

Across the Hawaiian Islands people built stone temples called heiau. Wickerwork structures represented their gods.

Ocean travel

The early Polynesians used their boats for fishing, trading, and to explore. The most common boats in the islands were canoes, which were built in many shapes and sizes. They could carry just one person or be 100 ft (30 m) long and capable of transporting up to 500 people over distances of more than 1,500 miles (2,500 km). Paddles were used for short distances, but sails were needed to catch the wind for long journeys.

LINE ISLANDS

KIRITIMATI

Dancers were accompanied by musicians playing drums, bamboo flutes, or shells.

Early colonists set out from Tonga and Samoa with men, women, children, animals, and seeds on their canoes.

TUVALU

PACIFIC OCEAN

SAMOA

Women wove baskets from the fronds of the coconut palm. The trunk provided timber for homes, and the leaves were used for thatch.

MARQUESAS ISLANDS

SOCIETY ISLANDS

Later Polynesians started to grow sweet potatoes, yams, taro, bananas, and breadfruit, and kept dogs, pigs, and chickens.

Two Māori warriors in a hand-to-hand duel. Each used a sharp-edged club made of whalebone or a type of jade called greenstone.

TONGA

COOK ISLANDS

TAHITI

Polynesians ate mainly seafood, yams, and fruit. Leaves were used as plates. Fish were caught by spear, net, or even by hand.

Pigs were sometimes sacrificed and placed on platforms as an offering to the gods.

PITCAIRN

Small canoes were used for travel between neighboring islands.

EASTER ISLAND

NEW ZEALAND

NORTH ISLAND

SOUTH ISLAND

CHATHAM ISLAND

Māori chiefs often had tattoo marks carved on their faces. They wore cloaks made of flax and kiwi feathers.

The largest islands

When the Polynesians (later called Māori) reached New Zealand, they found a land much colder and wetter than they were used to. The only familiar crop they could grow was a type of sweet potato. They hunted a large flightless bird, the moa, and relied on farming, fishing, and gathering. Māori families belonged to a tribe and were ruled by a chief, or *rangatira*. They worshiped the spirits of dead ancestors and also believed that certain people or places were sacred. These were called *tapu*, or taboo.

The Māori were expert woodcarvers. This sculpture shows one of their main ancestors, Pukaki, with his two sons.

From 1300 CE onward, the people of Easter Island set up 30-ft (10-m) tall stone statues.

| 0 | 500 | 1000 | 1500 Kilometers |

| 0 | 500 | 1000 Miles |

China—The Golden Age

CHINA WENT THROUGH many years of war following the death of the First Emperor. But by 626 CE, the country had settled into a new and golden age founded by the emperor Tang Taizong, first of the Tang dynasty of emperors. The capital city, now at Chang'an, became the center for traders who arrived on the Silk Road. Markets and bazaars buzzed with activity and many kinds of religion existed. For the first time ordinary people could get government jobs. The production of salt, paper, and iron also provided work. During this peaceful time arts and crafts flourished.

These hills in southern China were a favorite subject for painters.

In 751 CE Muslim forces defeated the Chinese at the Battle of Talas and the Chinese lost control of the Kashgar area.

Nomadic tribes on the northern frontier were a constant threat.

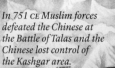

THE SILK ROAD

Camel caravans headed west along the Silk Road.

Tashkent

Kucha

Traders traveled in groups called caravans, resting overnight during the long journey along the Silk Road.

Samarkand

The Chinese monk Xuanzang returned from India in 645 CE with Buddhist texts for fellow students.

Kashgar

T A N G

THE SILK ROAD

Khotan

The good life

Wealthy people led a comfortable life. They wore silk clothes and entertained their friends with lavish feasts. Servants prepared meals of roasted pig and deer, washed down with drinks made from millet and rice. They listened to music and poetry, and played games such as chess and cards. People filled their homes with luxury goods made of gold, silver, jade, and porcelain. Paintings on silk and lacquerwork were popular.

This painting of a court lady shows how wealthy women would have dressed.

0   100   200   300   400 Kilometers

0   100   200   300 Miles

TRADE ROUTE TO INDIA

Great inventions

The Chinese were brilliant inventors. By the time of the Tang emperors they could make paper, and later they created printing using wooden blocks on paper. During the Tang dynasty they invented a mechanical water clock, a magnetic compass, and the fine porcelain that we still call "china."

This scene is from the world's oldest known printed book, the Diamond Sutra. It was printed in 868 CE.

The capital of Chang'an

Under the rule of the Tang emperors, the capital at Chang'an became the world's largest city. The name Chang'an means "Eternal Peace." The city had a population of more than one million, as well as many foreign traders, scholars, and travelers.

The emperor's palace was built in the northern part of the city.

Many soldiers were farmers who had to serve in the army.

Musicians and dancers performed to passers-by.

Buildings were made from wood covered with lacquer. Roofs were tiled.

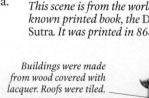

Anyone seeking a government job took an examination. The empress Wu included writing poetry in this test.

Farmers sold goods in the city's streets.

People wore silk robes. Only emperors could wear yellow.

A noble was carried on a chair called a palanquin.

The Chinese discovered gunpowder and created firecrackers.

Li Bai, the most famous poet of the day, came to the city to write for the emperor.

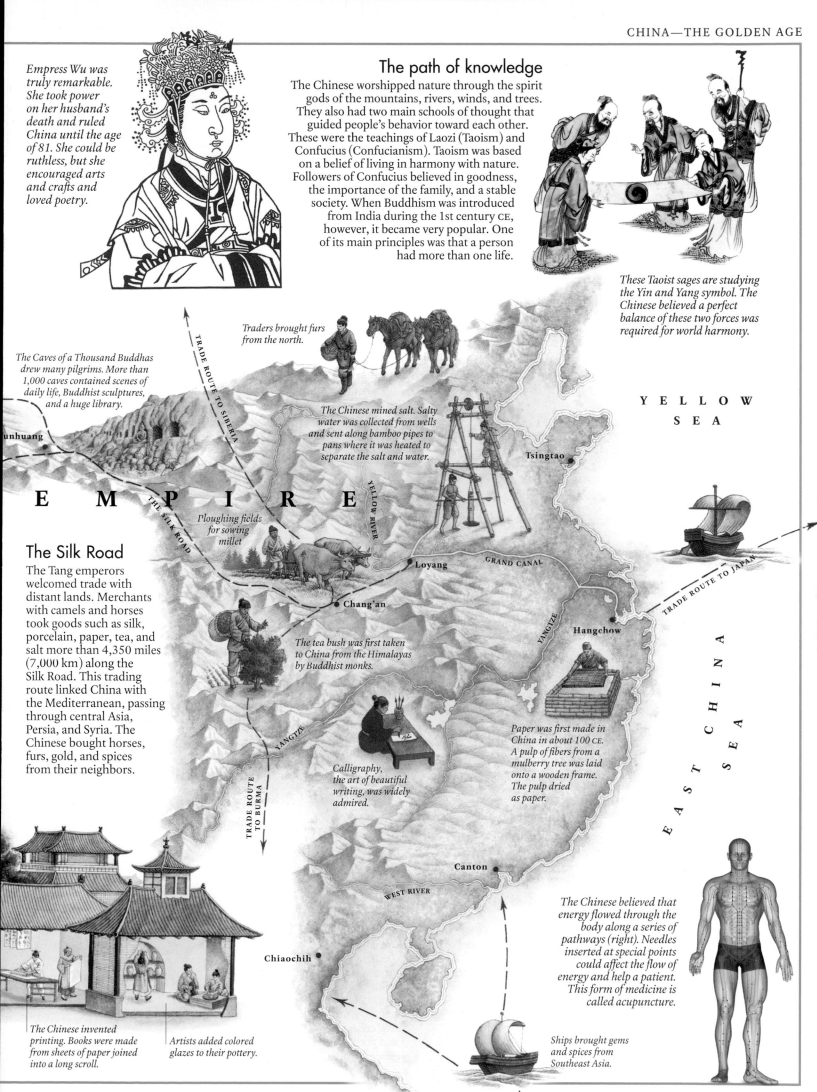

Empress Wu was truly remarkable. She took power on her husband's death and ruled China until the age of 81. She could be ruthless, but she encouraged arts and crafts and loved poetry.

The path of knowledge

The Chinese worshipped nature through the spirit gods of the mountains, rivers, winds, and trees. They also had two main schools of thought that guided people's behavior toward each other. These were the teachings of Laozi (Taoism) and Confucius (Confucianism). Taoism was based on a belief of living in harmony with nature. Followers of Confucius believed in goodness, the importance of the family, and a stable society. When Buddhism was introduced from India during the 1st century CE, however, it became very popular. One of its main principles was that a person had more than one life.

These Taoist sages are studying the Yin and Yang symbol. The Chinese believed a perfect balance of these two forces was required for world harmony.

Traders brought furs from the north.

The Caves of a Thousand Buddhas drew many pilgrims. More than 1,000 caves contained scenes of daily life, Buddhist sculptures, and a huge library.

Dunhuang

The Chinese mined salt. Salty water was collected from wells and sent along bamboo pipes to pans where it was heated to separate the salt and water.

YELLOW SEA

Tsingtao

TRADE ROUTE TO SIBERIA

E M P I R E

THE SILK ROAD

YELLOW RIVER

Ploughing fields for sowing millet

The Silk Road

The Tang emperors welcomed trade with distant lands. Merchants with camels and horses took goods such as silk, porcelain, paper, tea, and salt more than 4,350 miles (7,000 km) along the Silk Road. This trading route linked China with the Mediterranean, passing through central Asia, Persia, and Syria. The Chinese bought horses, furs, gold, and spices from their neighbors.

Loyang

GRAND CANAL

Chang'an

TRADE ROUTE TO JAPAN

The tea bush was first taken to China from the Himalayas by Buddhist monks.

YANGTZE

Hangchow

Paper was first made in China in about 100 CE. A pulp of fibers from a mulberry tree was laid onto a wooden frame. The pulp dried as paper.

YANGTZE

TRADE ROUTE TO BURMA

Calligraphy, the art of beautiful writing, was widely admired.

E A S T   C H I N A   S E A

Canton

WEST RIVER

The Chinese believed that energy flowed through the body along a series of pathways (right). Needles inserted at special points could affect the flow of energy and help a patient. This form of medicine is called acupuncture.

Chiaochih

The Chinese invented printing. Books were made from sheets of paper joined into a long scroll.

Artists added colored glazes to their pottery.

Ships brought gems and spices from Southeast Asia.

Japan—Rise of the Samurai

THE FIRST EMPEROR OF JAPAN was the legendary Jimmu Tenno, who was said to be descended from the Sun Goddess. At first the emperors of Japan ruled supreme. They owned all the land and kept order with an army of peasant soldiers. But during the Heian Period (794–1185 CE), the emperors gave so much land away to noble families, called clans, that they gradually became rich enough to set up their own armies.

In 858 CE, the powerful Fujiwara clan, while still respecting the emperor, took control of the government. For a while they ruled efficiently, but other clans challenged them. In 1192 CE, the Minamoto clan took over and the emperor appointed Minamoto Yoritomo as the first shogun, or military dictator. Under shogun rule, a class of warriors called samurai gained considerable power. For the next 700 years, Japan was ruled by shoguns and samurai.

The flowering of Japan

During the 6th century CE, Japan began to absorb ideas from its neighbor, China. Signs of these changes could be seen in the arts and architecture. Bronze statues of the Buddha appeared. Chinese-style houses with tiled roofs were built, and Chinese writing was adapted to create a new written language. Gradually all these new ideas were changed to suit Japanese tastes, developing a distinctive Japanese culture.

The Ainu, Japan's earliest people, created a dance said to keep bears away.

HOKKAIDO

PACIFIC OCEAN

Whales were hunted as a source of food.

In the 8th century CE, an imperial decree declared that the arrival of the cherry blossom would be celebrated each spring.

SEA OF JAPAN

Akita

Granaries were used to store rice, a key Japanese crop since 300 BCE.

JAPAN

Fujisan—Mount Fuji—is the sacred mountain of Japan.

Chinese envoys, craftworkers, and Buddhist monks crossed to Japan.

Lady Murasaki Shikibu wrote the Tale of Genji in 1007 CE. The book, more than 600,000 words long, is one of the world's first novels.

HONSHU

The way of the warrior

Samurai were prominent during the troubled 10th and 11th centuries. They protected the lands of the *daimyo* (local lords) and had a strict code of honor known as *bushido*, meaning "way of the warrior." As a battle began, each samurai announced his name and those of his ancestors, challenging opponents to fight. They fought bravely and preferred to die rather than accept defeat. Samurai were expert horsemen, able to shoot arrows accurately from a fast-moving horse.

Izumi was one of many Shinto shrines dedicated to the Sun Goddess.

Izumo

Heian-kyo (Kyoto)

Kamakura

Nara

Minamoto Yoritomo fought the powerful Taira clan in the Gempei War (1180–1185 CE). In 1192 CE, he was made shogun, the emperor's chief of military affairs.

SHIKOKU

Nara, the first capital of Japan, was the site of the Buddhist temple of Horyu-ji.

KYUSHU

Divers searched for pearls in the Pacific Ocean.

The bow and arrow was the early samurai's chief weapon.

Early samurai warrior

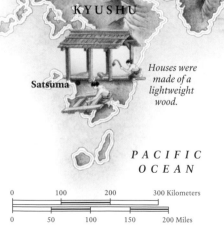

Samurai wore helmets in battle.

Armor was made from strips of tough leather.

Satsuma

Houses were made of a lightweight wood.

The court at Kyoto

In 794 CE, the Japanese capital moved from Nara to Heian-kyo (later called Kyoto). The new capital was beautiful, and the courtiers, who were known as "dwellers among the clouds," lived in luxury. They filled their days with walks in the gardens, beautiful objects, writing letters and poems, and attending court and temple ceremonies.

The best horses were from the mountains of northern Japan.

Swords were made from high-quality steel.

PACIFIC OCEAN

| 0 | 100 | 200 | 300 Kilometers |
| 0 | 50 | 100 | 150 | 200 Miles |

Kingdom of the Khmers

THE TEMPLE CITIES of Angkor dominated the plain where the people known as Khmers flourished for more than 600 years. The Khmer kingdom, in modern-day Cambodia, first rose to power under King Jayavarman II, who ruled from 802–835 CE. After years of trading with India, the Khmers adopted many aspects of Indian culture, especially the Hindu religion and ornate Indian architecture.

Jayavarman II proclaimed himself a god king with power bestowed on him by the Hindu god Shiva. From then on, Khmer kings built temples for their gods and fine palaces for themselves, and life for most Khmers came to be devoted to serving their god king. Engineers devised a system of irrigation so that farmers could grow enough to feed the priests, courtiers, and craftworkers who lived in and around the temple palaces.

In 1431 CE, the Siamese invaded Cambodia and sacked Angkor Wat, ending the Khmer empire. The Khmers retreated south to Phnom Penh.

The king appeared twice daily at a golden window to conduct business and hear people's complaints.

When the Tonle Sap lake flooded each year, men scooped up baskets of fish. Many families lived in stilted thatch homes around the lake.

Elephants were used to move heavy loads and for hunting.

This huge stone head shows one of the four faces of Jayavarman VII (1181–1218 CE), who drove out the invading Chams and rebuilt the city of Angkor. Unlike other Khmer kings, he was a Buddhist, not a Hindu.

ANNAM

MEKONG

MUN

CHAO PHRAYA

SIAM

Koh Ker

KHMER KINGDOM

Angkor

Roluos

TONLE SAP

Preah Khan

CHAMPA

Binh Dinh

SOUTH CHINA SEA

Buddhism did not become popular until the 12th century CE.

Figures of celestial dancers, called apsaras, were carved into the walls of Angkor Wat to entertain the gods.

GULF OF SIAM

Indravarman I organized a network of reservoirs for irrigating the rice fields.

0   50   100   150 Kilometers
0   50   100 Miles

MEKONG

Phnom Penh

In 1177 CE, the Chams launched a surprise attack by sailing up the Mekong River to Angkor. They were later driven out by King Jayavarman VII.

A Chinese envoy, Zhou Daguan, sailed to Angkor in 1296 CE. He wrote detailed accounts of what he saw.

Saigon

Peacock feathers were highly prized.

Oc Eo

FUNAN

Scholars wrote on sections of palm leaf.

Waters of life

Water was vital for life. From May to October each year, the monsoon rains caused the Mekong River to flood. When the waters receded, the fertile plain was used to grow rice. Rainwater was stored in reservoirs and canals to irrigate the fields during the rest of the year. Water was also needed because in the hot weather people bathed a few times a day. Archaeologists have found the remains of several palace pools.

The naga was a mythical snake, based on the cobra of Hindu mythology, that represented the kindly, life-giving spirit of the water.

Angkor Wat

Angkor Wat, meaning "city temple," was built in 1113 CE by Suryavarman II. It was a combination of temples and palaces where the god kings lived and were buried. The buildings were decorated with relief sculptures showing mythical scenes of Hindu gods, the Khmers at war, and royal processions. Angkor Wat was surrounded by a massive moat and the causeway leading to the temple was lined with images of seven-headed *nagas*.

The temple of Angkor Wat was uncovered in 1861 by French naturalist Henri Mouhot. Earlier visitors had reported seeing a "lost city" in the jungle.

Maya—Cities of Stone

THE RUINS of spectacular stone cities rise above the tropical forests of Mesoamerica. Royal cities such as Tikal, Palenque, and Copán became home to people known as the Maya, who were at their most creative between 250 and 900 CE. The lands of the Maya were divided into several kingdoms, each ruled by a godlike king. Every kingdom had a capital city that controlled the towns, villages, and farmlands around it.

Farmers grew maize, beans, and squash, and hunters trapped rabbit, iguana, and deer.

To impress their subjects and fellow rulers, kings enriched their cities with monuments decorated with elaborate carvings and paintings. The Maya were also clever astronomers and mathematicians. They developed a sophisticated calendar and method of counting, and invented a system of writing with picture signs, called glyphs, that tells us about the kings and their conquests.

Carved in stone

Mayan cities were vast complexes with multistory buildings, temple-topped pyramids, and ballcourts, grouped around a central plaza. Construction of the cities must have been quite a task as the Maya had no metal for tools until later. Builders used obsidian, a rock from the solid lava of the region's volcanoes, to carve limestone blocks. Artists used a local red dye for decoration.

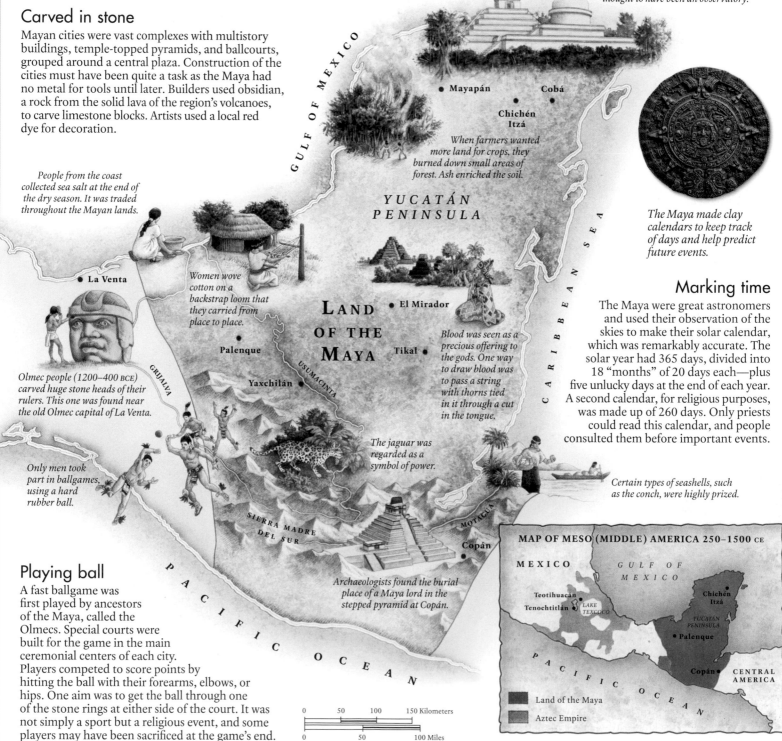

Chichén Itzá was one of the later Mayan cities, built between 750 and 1200 CE. The building in the foreground is thought to have been an observatory.

People from the coast collected sea salt at the end of the dry season. It was traded throughout the Mayan lands.

When farmers wanted more land for crops, they burned down small areas of forest. Ash enriched the soil.

• Mayapán   • Cobá

• Chichén Itzá

YUCATÁN PENINSULA

GULF OF MEXICO

CARIBBEAN SEA

The Maya made clay calendars to keep track of days and help predict future events.

• La Venta

Women wove cotton on a backstrap loom that they carried from place to place.

LAND OF THE MAYA

• El Mirador

Olmec people (1200–400 BCE) carved huge stone heads of their rulers. This one was found near the old Olmec capital of La Venta.

• Palenque

Tikal •

Blood was seen as a precious offering to the gods. One way to draw blood was to pass a string with thorns tied in it through a cut in the tongue.

• Yaxchilán

GRIJALVA

USUMACINTA

The jaguar was regarded as a symbol of power.

Only men took part in ballgames, using a hard rubber ball.

SIERRA MADRE DEL SUR

MOTAGUA

• Copán

Certain types of seashells, such as the conch, were highly prized.

Marking time

The Maya were great astronomers and used their observation of the skies to make their solar calendar, which was remarkably accurate. The solar year had 365 days, divided into 18 "months" of 20 days each—plus five unlucky days at the end of each year. A second calendar, for religious purposes, was made up of 260 days. Only priests could read this calendar, and people consulted them before important events.

Archaeologists found the burial place of a Maya lord in the stepped pyramid at Copán.

PACIFIC OCEAN

Playing ball

A fast ballgame was first played by ancestors of the Maya, called the Olmecs. Special courts were built for the game in the main ceremonial centers of each city. Players competed to score points by hitting the ball with their forearms, elbows, or hips. One aim was to get the ball through one of the stone rings at either side of the court. It was not simply a sport but a religious event, and some players may have been sacrificed at the game's end.

0   50   100   150 Kilometers

0   50   100 Miles

MAP OF MESO (MIDDLE) AMERICA 250–1500 CE

MEXICO   **GULF OF MEXICO**

• Teotihuacan

Tenochtitlán •   LAKE TEXCOCO

YUCATÁN PENINSULA

• Chichén Itzá

• Palenque

Copán •   **CENTRAL AMERICA**

PACIFIC OCEAN

■ Land of the Maya

■ Aztec Empire

Aztecs—Warriors of the Sun

THE AZTECS were a fierce tribe of warriors who settled in the Valley of Mexico in the 13th century CE. They fought endless wars with neighboring tribes until they dominated most of middle America. Like the Maya and Toltecs before them, they built spectacular cities. Their capital city at Tenochtitlán—where Mexico City now stands—lay on an island in Lake Texcoco, and around 200,000 Aztecs, or Mexica as they called themselves, lived there. Within the city wall there were palaces, pyramids, and temples where priests carried out human sacrifices as part of a religious ritual to nourish the gods. The Aztecs believed they had to please their gods or the world would end.

The handle of this sacrificial knife is inlaid with precious turquoise and shell.

Trade and treasure

The Aztecs grew rich by collecting payment from conquered tribes. Cloth, maize, and luxury items were brought to Tenochtitlán from defeated cities. Goods were also acquired by trade. Merchants called *pochteca* traveled all over the empire to bring back gold, silver, and tin as well as precious stones of jade, turquoise, amethyst, and amber. Brightly colored feathers from exotic birds—quetzals and parrots—were also brought back to make cloaks and headdresses. Scribes kept detailed lists of the treasures taken from conquered cities.

Aztec warriors

To keep their empire strong, all Aztec boys were trained to become warriors. When a boy reached the age of 10, his hair was cut, leaving a tuft of hair at the back. When he captured his first prisoner, the tuft of hair was cut. The best fighters became jaguar warriors and wore jaguar skins into battle, or they became eagle warriors and dressed with an eagle's head helmet.

Quetzalcoatl, a Toltec god, was also worshipped by the Aztecs.

Sacrifice was important to Aztec religion. Human hearts were offered to the Sun God.

GULF OF MEXICO

• Tula

Tlacopán
Tenochtitlán

Texcoco •
LAKE
TEXCOCO

The emperor Moctezuma was carried on a litter. Ordinary people could not look at him.

• Cempoala

Spanish invaders, led by Hernán Cortés, landed at Cempoala in 1519 CE.

AZTEC EMPIRE

BALSAS

Aztec warriors used a sling to hurl their spears at speed.

Food grew on reclaimed swamp land (chinampas).

Cacao beans were used to make a luxury drink, chocolate. The beans were so valuable that they were used as money.

A daring ritual saw four men, tied by their ankles, swing out around a pole.

• Mitla

The main crop of maize was stored above ground in a special granary.

Scribes painted symbols onto bark, which was folded into a book called a codex. This page shows items taken as tribute.

PACIFIC OCEAN

The Aztecs had no wheeled vehicles or strong pack animals. All trade goods were carried by porters.

TRADE ROUTE TO
CENTRAL AMERICA

| 0 | 25 | 50 | 75 Kilometers |
| 0 | 25 | | 50 Miles |

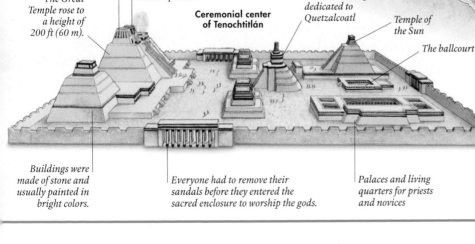

Temple of Tlaloc

Temple of Huitzilopochtli

The Great Temple rose to a height of 200 ft (60 m).

Ceremonial center of Tenochtitlán

The round temple, dedicated to Quetzalcoatl

Temple of the Sun

The ballcourt

Buildings were made of stone and usually painted in bright colors.

Everyone had to remove their sandals before they entered the sacred enclosure to worship the gods.

Palaces and living quarters for priests and novices

The floating city

Tenochtitlán was built on a swamp in Lake Texcoco and connected to the mainland by three wide causeways, or roads. At the city's heart a ceremonial center was dominated by the Great Temple. At the top of a flight of steps there were two smaller temples—one dedicated to Huitzilopochtli, a sun and war god, and the other to the rain god Tlaloc. In 1519 CE Spanish conquistadors (conquerors) invaded Mexico. Within two years they had destroyed the Aztec empire.

Inca—Lords of the Andes

THE INCA EMPIRE was a land of contrasts, dominated by the mountain range of the snowcapped Andes. Several cultures had flourished here—the Chavín, Moche, Nazca, and Chimú—but the greatest of all were the Inca. By about 1200 CE the Inca had grown into an organized society united under one ruler, the Sapa Inca. From his capital at Cusco, he was worshipped as a living god. In 1438 CE, the ruling Inca, Pachachuti Yupanqui, set out on a plan of conquest. Within a few years the Inca had an empire that stretched 2,200 miles (3,500 km) along South America's Pacific coast, covering much of modern Ecuador, Peru, Bolivia, and Chile.

Machu Picchu was an important fortress city, perched high in the Andes. It escaped the notice of the Spanish conquerors and was not rediscovered until 1911.

The Inca

Inca rulers were thought to be descended from the sun god, Inti, so had absolute power. The eighth Inca ruler, Viracocha, took the title Sapa ("Supreme") Inca, or Emperor. The emperor dressed in specially woven clothes and wore golden discs in his ears. To keep the sun's blood pure, he married his sister. The sister-wife was called Coya, or Empress. An emperor had many wives, but only a Coya's son could be the next emperor.

The fortress at Cusco, below, was made of tightly fitted stone blocks. In an earthquake, they shifted then fell back into place.

Capital Cusco

Cusco grew from a small village into a capital city. Its layout was said to be shaped like a puma, with the fortress of Sacsahuamán forming the head. At its center was the Haucaypata, or Holy Place, where important ceremonies were held. There were also royal palaces and temples. The Temple of the sun had a garden with life-size llamas, birds, and ears of corn made of gold and silver.

This gold and turquoise knife ornament of a richly dressed man was made by the Chimú people whose capital city was at Chan Chan.

Women made a drink called chicha by chewing corn into a pulp. They spat the pulp into water and sieved it into jars.

The alpaca's fine wool was used to make warm clothing.

The Spaniard Francisco Pizarro arrived in 1532 CE, with a 200-strong army. Within a few years, they had destroyed the mighty Inca Empire.

The Chimú people's expansion threatened the Inca Empire, so the Inca prince Yupanqui invaded, destroyed their fortress, and took their ruler captive.

Young women were chosen to live in convents of the sun where they spun and wove wool for the emperor's clothes.

In November, the month of the dead, the mummified bodies of past emperors were carried in procession.

The Inca made bridges from rope to cross deep chasms in the mountains.

The road builders

The Inca built an impressive network of paved foot roads, overcoming incredible natural obstacles. They built stone bridges and suspension bridges made from twisted vines. Along the roads they built rest houses, called *tambos*. Two runners were stationed at each *tambo* ready to relay messages to Cusco from across the empire. A team of runners could cover 150 miles (240 km) a day.

Map labels: Quito, Tomebamba, Chan Chan, MARANON, Jauja, Pachacámac, Cusco, Machu Picchu, Vilcashuamán, Nazca, INCA ROAD, ANDES, INCA EMPIRE, LAKE TITICACA, PACIFIC

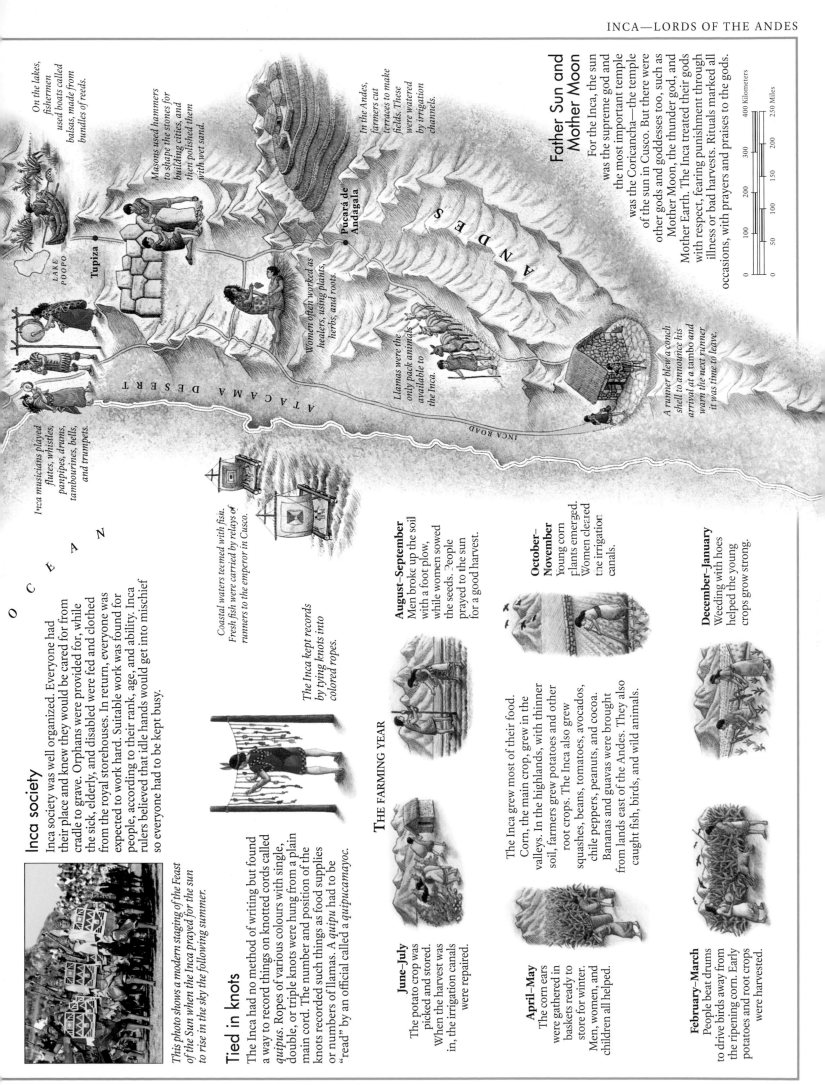

On the lakes, fishermen used boats called balsas, made from bundles of reeds.

Masons used hammers to shape the stones for building cities, and then polished them with wet sand.

In the Andes, farmers cut terraces to make fields. These were watered by irrigation channels.

Father Sun and Mother Moon

For the Inca, the sun was the supreme god and the most important temple was the Coricancha—the temple of the sun in Cusco. But there were other gods and goddesses too, such as Mother Moon, the thunder god, and Mother Earth. The Inca treated their gods with respect, fearing punishment through illness or bad harvests. Rituals marked all occasions, with prayers and praises to the gods.

400 Kilometers
250 Miles

LAKE POOPO

Tupiza

Pucará de Andagala

Women often worked as healers, using plants, herbs, and roots.

A N D E S

Llamas were the only pack animals available to the Inca.

A runner blew a conch shell to announce his arrival at a tambo and warn the next runner it was time to leave.

INCA ROAD

A T A C A M A   D E S E R T

O C E A N

Inca musicians played flutes, whistles, panpipes, drums, tambourines, bells, and trumpets.

This photo shows a modern staging of the Feast of the Sun when the Inca prayed for the sun to rise in the sky the following summer.

Inca society

Inca society was well organized. Everyone had their place and knew they would be cared for from cradle to grave. Orphans were provided for, while the sick, elderly, and disabled were fed and clothed from the royal storehouses. In return, everyone was expected to work hard. Suitable work was found for people, according to their rank, age, and ability. Inca rulers believed that idle hands would get into mischief so everyone had to be kept busy.

Tied in knots

The Inca had no method of writing but found a way to record things on knotted cords called *quipus*. Ropes of various colours with single, double, or triple knots were hung from a plain main cord. The number and position of the knots recorded such things as food supplies or numbers of llamas. A *quipu* had to be "read" by an official called a *quipucamayoc*.

Coastal waters teemed with fish. Fresh fish were carried by relays of runners to the emperor in Cusco.

The Inca kept records by tying knots into colored ropes.

THE FARMING YEAR

August–September
Men broke up the soil with a foot plow, while women sowed the seeds. People prayed to the sun for a good harvest.

October–November
Young corn plants emerged. Women cleared the irrigation canals.

December–January
Weeding with hoes helped the young crops grow strong.

The Inca grew most of their food. Corn, the main crop, grew in the valleys. In the highlands, with thinner soil, farmers grew potatoes and other root crops. The Inca also grew squashes, beans, tomatoes, avocados, chile peppers, peanuts, and cocoa. Bananas and guavas were brought from lands east of the Andes. They also caught fish, birds, and wild animals.

June–July
The potato crop was picked and stored. When the harvest was in, the irrigation canals were repaired.

April–May
The corn ears were gathered in baskets ready to store for winter. Men, women, and children all helped.

February–March
People beat drums to drive birds away from the ripening corn. Early potatoes and root crops were harvested.

Time Chart

THIS TIME CHART summarizes the major events, battles, personalities, and inventions that are covered in this book. Entries have been organized in date order so that you can trace the rise and fall of different civilizations and also find out what was happening elsewhere in the world at the same time. Illustrations highlight some of the important rulers, architectural wonders, and events featured in the book.

c.2500 BCE Rise of Indus Valley civilization in India and Pakistan.
c.2500 BCE Mesopotamians develop units for weights and measures.
c.2500 BCE Central Asian people tame horses.
2500–2000 BCE Spread of Beaker people throughout northern Europe.
c.2350 BCE Sargon unites cities of Akkad and then conquers Sumer.
2300 BCE Earliest surviving map on baked clay tablet from Babylon.
c.2300 BCE Pottery in use in Mexico and Guatemala.
c.2130–1633 BCE Middle Kingdom in Egypt.

Great Bath at Mohenjo-Daro, Indus Valley

Sargon of Akkad

c.2100 BCE The great ziggurat (temple tower) built at Ur in Sumer.
c.2000 BCE Settlement of Pacific islands of Melanesia by immigrants from Indonesia.

Building a step pyramid, Egypt

c.3000 BCE Agriculture in use in Mexico and Peru.
c.3000 BCE Spread of megalith tombs across Europe.
2900 BCE Port of Byblos founded in Phoenicia.
c.2750 BCE Royal graves are dug at Ur in Sumer.
2686–2181 BCE Old Kingdom in Egypt.
2650 BCE Step pyramid built at Saqqara in Egypt.

c.1028 BCE Shang Dynasty in China overthrown by Zhou Dynasty.
1020 BCE Kingdom of Israel is established.
c.1000 BCE Phoenicians produce simple alphabet, the basis of the alphabet we use today.
c.1000 BCE In Australia, long-distance trade networks used for the exchange of ornaments and raw materials.
c.1000 BCE Iron in use in Aegean and central Europe.
c.1000 BCE Lapita settlers are established on Tonga and Samoa.

Phoenician traders

c.922 BCE King Solomon dies; kingdom of Israel split into Judah and Israel.
c.911–612 BCE New Assyrian Empire.
c.900 BCE Rise of Chavin culture in Peru.
c.900 BCE City of Carthage founded by Phoenicians in North Africa.
c.900 BCE Etruscan civilization emerges in northern Italy.

Bull leaping ceremony, Crete

c.2000–1450 BCE Minoans build large palaces on Crete, including Knossos, Phaistos, and Mallia.
c.2000 BCE Hittite states are set up in Anatolia.
c.2000 BCE End of Sumer and Akkad.
c.2000 BCE Skis are shown on Swedish rock carving.
c.2000 BCE Shadow clocks are in use by Egyptians.
c.2000 BCE Sumer is invaded by Amorites.

Sumerian scribes

c.3250 BCE Cuneiform writing develops in Sumer.
c.3200 BCE The wheel is invented in Sumer and used to make pottery and to move carts and chariots.
c.3000 BCE Cochise hunter-gatherers are living in southwest North America.

Bronze worker

c.2000 BCE Start of the Bronze Age in western Asia.
1814–1363 BCE First Assyrian Empire.
c.1800 BCE First horse-drawn war chariot in the Middle East.

1200 BCE Eastern Mediterranean invaded by the Sea Peoples.
c.1200–1000 BCE Phoenicians rise to power.
c.1150 BCE Destruction of Mycenaean civilization; start of Dark Ages in Greece.

Sea Peoples

New Kingdom pharaoh

1323 BCE New Kingdom pharaoh Tutankhamun buried in the Valley of the Kings, Egypt.
c.1250 BCE Legendary Trojan War fought between the Mycenaeans and the Trojans.
c.1200 BCE Development of Urnfield culture, ancestors of the Celts, in central Europe.
c.1200 BCE Hebrews return to Canaan from Egypt.

Queen of Sheba visits Solomon

c.900 BCE The Rig Veda, a collection of 1,000 sacred hymns, is composed in India.
c.814 BCE City of Carthage founded by Phoenicians in North Africa.
c.776 BCE First Olympic Games held in Greece.

Assyrian winged bull

c.753 BCE Founding of city of Rome.
c.750 BCE Celtic culture starts to develop around Hallstatt, Austria.
c.705 BCE Assyrian King Sennacherib makes Nineveh his capital.

King Hammurabi of Babylon records his laws

c.1800–900 BCE Initial Period in Peru. People settle in villages.
1792–1750 BCE Reign of King Hammurabi of Babylon.

City of Ugarit, Canaan

Mycenaean death mask

1450 BCE Mycenaeans invade Crete.
c.1363–1047 BCE Middle Assyrian Empire.

Stonehenge, England

c.1500 BCE Collapse of Indus Valley civilization.
c.1500 BCE The Lapita people, ancestors of the Polynesians, expand outward from Indonesia.
c.1500 BCE–200 CE Olmec culture in Mexico.

Persian palace, Persepolis

671 BCE Egypt conquered by Assyria.
c.612–539 BCE Babylonian Empire dominates the Middle East.
c.600 BC Adena people farming and building burial mounds in North America.
c.563–483 BCE Life of Siddhartha Gautama, the Buddha.
551–479 BCE Life of Confucius.
c.550 BCE Pythagoras develops his mathematical theorem.
549 BCE Rise of Persian Empire under King Cyrus.

Terracotta Nok head

c.1700 BCE Canaanites use a new way of writing—an alphabet of 27 letters.
1650 BCE Rise of the Hittite Kingdom in Anatolia.
1650 BCE Rise of city-state of Mycenae in Greece.
c.1600 BCE Building of Stonehenge in England is completed.
c.1595 BCE Babylonia invaded by Kassites.
1567–1069 BCE New Kingdom in Egypt.
c.1500–1028 BCE Shang Dynasty in China.
c.1500 BCE Deir el-Medina, the village for craftworkers who built the Egyptian royal tombs, is founded.
c.1500 BCE Wet-rice agriculture begins in Korea.
c.1500 BCE Cattle and goats domesticated in West Africa.

c.524–404 BCE Egypt conquered and occupied by Persia.
c.500 BCE Kingdom of Meroë, under kings of Napata, rises to power in northeast Africa.
c.500 BCE Start of Nok culture in modern-day Nigeria.
c.500 BCE First coins in China.
c.500 BCE Celtic La Tène culture in Europe.
c.500 BCE First copper smelting in West Africa.
c.490 BCE Defeat of Persian King Darius at the Battle of Marathon.

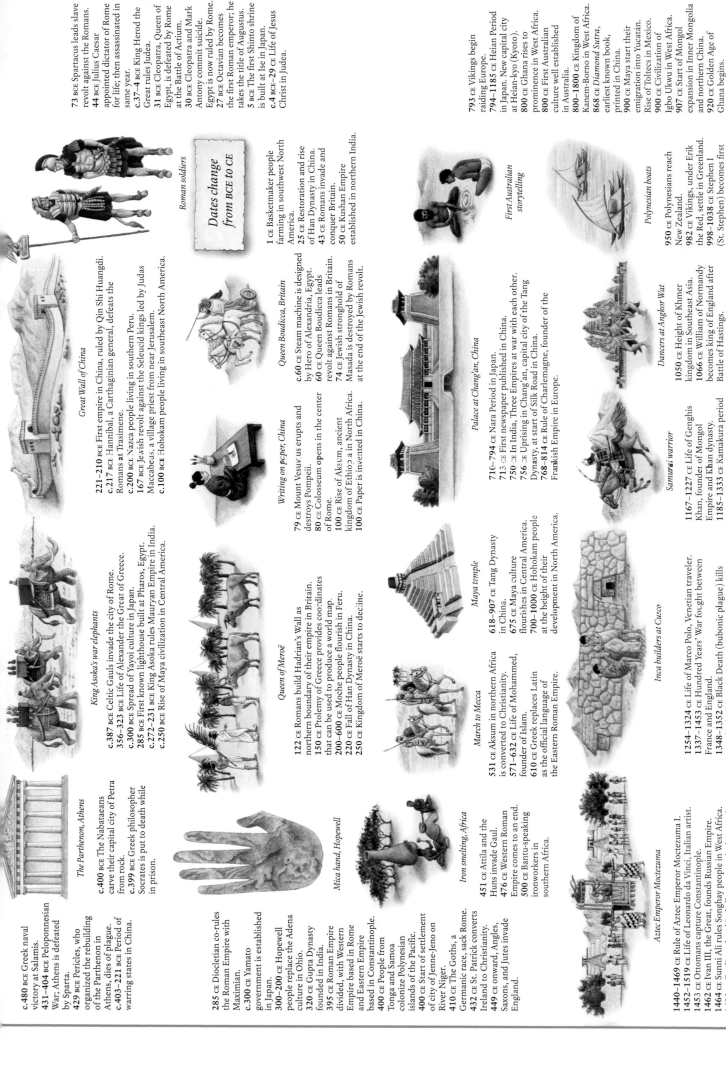

The Parthenon, Athens

c.480 BCE Greek naval victory at Salamis.
431–404 BCE Peloponnesian War; Athens is defeated by Sparta.
429 BCE Pericles, who organized the rebuilding of the Parthenon in Athens, dies of plague.
c.403–221 BCE Period of warring states in China.

c.400 BCE The Nabataeans carve their capital city of Petra from rock.
c.399 BCE Greek philosopher Socrates is put to death while in prison.

King Asoka's war elephants

c.387 BCE Celtic Gauls invade the city of Rome.
356–323 BCE Life of Alexander the Great of Greece.
c.300 BCE Spread of Yayoi culture in Japan.
285 BCE First known lighthouse built at Pharos, Egypt.
c.272–231 BCE King Asoka rules Mauryan Empire in India.
c.250 BCE Rise of Maya civilization in Central America.

Great Wall of China

221–210 BCE First empire in China, ruled by Qin Shi Huangdi.
c.217 BCE Hannibal, a Carthaginian general, defeats the Romans at Trasimene.
c.200 BCE Nazca people living in southern Peru.
167 BCE Jewish revolt against the Seleucid kings led by Judas Maccabeus, a village priest from near Jerusalem.
c.100 BCE Hohokam people living in southeast North America.

Roman soldiers

73 BCE Spartacus leads slave revolt against the Romans.
44 BCE Julius Caesar appointed dictator of Rome for life; then assassinated in same year.
c.37–4 BCE King Herod the Great rules Judea.
31 BCE Cleopatra, Queen of Egypt, is defeated by Rome at the Battle of Actium.
30 BCE Cleopatra and Mark Antony commit suicide. Egypt is now ruled by Rome.
27 BCE Octavian becomes the first Roman emperor; he takes the title of Augustus.
5 BCE The first Shinto shrine is built at Ise in Japan.
c.4 BCE–29 CE Life of Jesus Christ in Judea.

Dates change from BCE to CE

1 CE Basketmaker people farming in southwest North America.
25 CE Restoration and rise of Han Dynasty in China.
43 CE Romans invade and conquer Britain.
50 CE Kushan Empire established in northern India.

Queen Boudicca, Britain

c.60 CE Steam machine is designed by Hero of Alexandria, Egypt.
60 CE Queen Boudicca leads revolt against Romans in Britain.
74 CE Jewish stronghold of Masada is destroyed by Romans at the end of the Jewish revolt.

Writing on paper, China

79 CE Mount Vesuvius erupts and destroys Pompeii.
80 CE Colosseum opens in the center of Rome.
100 CE Rise of Aksum, ancient kingdom of Ethiopia in North Africa.
100 CE Paper is invented in China.

Queen of Meroë

122 CE Romans build Hadrian's Wall as northern boundary of their empire in Britain.
150 CE Ptolemy of Greece provides coordinates that can be used to produce a world map.
200–600 CE Moche people flourish in Peru.
220 CE Fall of Han Dynasty in China.
250 CE Kingdom of Meroë starts to decline.

Mica hand, Hopewell

285 CE Diocletian co-rules the Roman Empire with Maximian.
c.300 CE Yamato government is established in Japan.
320 CE Gupta Dynasty founded in India.
395 CE Roman Empire divided, with Western Empire based in Rome and Eastern Empire based in Constantinople.
400 CE People from Tonga and Samoa colonize Polynesian islands of the Pacific.
400 CE Start of settlement of city of Jenne-Jeno on River Niger.
410 CE The Goths, a Germanic race, sack Rome.
432 CE St. Patrick converts Ireland to Christianity.
449 CE onward, Angles, Saxons, and Jutes invade England.

Iron smelting, Africa

451 CE Attila and the Huns invade Gaul.
476 CE Western Roman Empire comes to an end.
500 CE Bantu-speaking ironworkers in southern Africa.

March to Mecca

531 CE Aksum in northern Africa is converted to Christianity.
571–632 CE Life of Mohammed, founder of Islam.
610 CE Greek replaces Latin as the official language of the Eastern Roman Empire.

Maya temple

618–907 CE Tang Dynasty in China.
675 CE Maya culture flourishes in Central America.
700–1000 CE Hohokam people at the height of their development in North America.

Palace at Chang'an, China

710–794 CE Nara Period in Japan.
713 CE First newspaper published in China.
750 CE In India, Three Empires at war with each other.
756 CE Uprising in Chang'an, capital city of the Tang Dynasty, at start of Silk Road in China.
768–814 CE Rule of Charlemagne, founder of the Frankish Empire in Europe.

First Australian storytelling

793 CE Vikings begin raiding Europe.
794–1185 CE Heian Period in Japan. New capital city at Heian-kyo (Kyoto).
800 CE Ghana rises to prominence in West Africa.
800 CE First Australian culture well established in Australia.
800–1800 CE Kingdom of Kanem-Borno in West Africa.
868 CE Diamond Sutra, earliest known book, printed in China.
900 CE Maya start their emigration into Yucatán. Rise of Toltecs in Mexico.
900 CE Civilization of Igbo Ukwu in West Africa.
907 CE Start of Mongol expansion in Inner Mongolia and northern China.
920 CE Golden Age of Ghana begins.

Polynesian boats

950 CE Polynesians reach New Zealand.
982 CE Vikings, under Erik the Red, settle in Greenland.
998–1038 CE Stephen I (St. Stephen) becomes first king of Hungary.
1000 CE Gunpowder in use in China.
1016 CE Cnut, Danish king, becomes king of England.

Dancers at Angkor Wat

1050 CE Height of Khmer kingdom in Southeast Asia.
1066 CE William of Normandy becomes king of England after Battle of Hastings.
1096 CE First Crusade to the Holy Land. Christians capture Jerusalem from the Muslims.
1100 CE Rise of kingdom of Ife in modern-day Nigeria.

Samurai warrior

1167–1227 CE Life of Genghis Khan, founder of Mongol Empire and Khan dynasty.
1185–1333 CE Kamakura period in Japan and rise of samurai.
1187 CE Muslim leader Saladin recaptures Jerusalem.
1215 CE Signing of Magna Carta by King John of England.

Inca builders at Cusco

1254–1324 CE Life of Marco Polo, Venetian traveler.
1337–1453 CE Hundred Years' War fought between France and England.
1348–1352 CE Black Death (bubonic plague) kills one-third of the population of Europe.
1368 CE Foundation of Ming Dynasty in China.
1369–1405 CE Tamerlane rules the Mongols.
1431 CE Joan of Arc burned at the stake in France.
1438 CE Inca Empire at its height in Peru.

Aztec Emperor Moctezuma

1440–1469 CE Rule of Aztec Emperor Moctezuma I.
1452–1519 CE Life of Leonardo da Vinci, Italian artist.
1453 CE Ottomans capture Constantinople.
1462 CE Ivan III, the Great, founds Russian Empire.
1464 CE Sunni Ali rules Songhay people in West Africa.
1492 CE Ferdinand and Isabella conquer the last Muslim stronghold in Spain.
1492 CE Christopher Columbus reaches the West Indies.
1501 CE Italian Amerigo Vespucci (who gave his name to the American continents) explores the coast of Brazil.

Index

ACKNOWLEDGMENTS

Dorling Kindersley would like to thank the following: Lynn Bresler for help with the Time Chart; Peter Bull and Richard Ward for additional artwork; Michelle de Larrabeiti for research; Hussain Mohamed for design assistance; Deepak Negi for picture research assistance; Caroline Stamps for editorial assistance.

Map consultant Roger Bullen
Picture research Diana Morris
Locator globes John Woodcock
Index Lynn Bresler

The publisher would like to thank the following for their kind permission to reproduce their photographs:
(Key: a-above; b-below/bottom; c-center; f-far; l-left; r-right; t-top)

4 Dreamstime.com: Yuri Yavnik (bc). **Getty Images:** Werner Forman / Universal Images Group (c). **5 Alamy Stock Photo:** World History Archive (bc). **6 Alamy Stock Photo:** Images & Stories (tr). **Photo Scala, Florence:** (bl). **8 Alamy Stock Photo:** CPA Media Pte Ltd (c); GRANGER – Historical Picture Archive (c). **Dorling Kindersley:** University of Aberdeen (cla). **Dreamstime.com:** Rafal Cichawa (br). **9 Alamy Stock Photo:**

fotolincs (cb). **Dorling Kindersley:** Geoff Brightling / St Thomas Hospital (clb); Newcastle Great Northern Museum, Hancock (tl). **10 Alamy Stock Photo:** INTERFOTO (crb). **SuperStock:** Pictures From History / Universal Images Group (tl). **Photo Scala, Florence:** (ca). **12 Dreamstime.com:** Sergii Kolesnyk (tr). **13 Alamy Stock Photo:** The Picture Art Collection (tl); Eye Ubiquitous (br). **14 Alamy Stock Photo:** agefotostock (ca); robertharding (cr). **Bridgeman Images:** (bc, bl). **Dreamstime.com:** Jiawangkun (c). **15 Bridgeman Images:** Werner Forman Archive (tr). **Getty Images:** Kitti Boonnitrod (cr). **Robert Harding Picture Library:** Robert Harding Productions (br). **16 Alamy Stock Photo:** Suzuki Kaku (tr). **17 Alamy Stock Photo:** The Print Collector (c). **Dreamstime.com:** Jason Wong (crb). **Getty Images:** Angelo Hornak / Corbis (ca). **19 Alamy Stock Photo:** World History Archive (br). **Dorling Kindersley:** Board of Trustees of the Royal Armouries (tl). **21 Alamy Stock Photo:** Hercules Milas (cb); VPC Travel Photo (cra). **© The Trustees of the British Museum. All rights reserved:** (br). **22 Alamy Stock Photo:** GRANGER – Historical Picture Archive (crb); www.BibleLand.Pictures.com (clb); EyeEm (ca). **24 Alamy Stock Photo:** funkyfood London – Paul Williams (tr); Jose Manuel Revuelta Luna (ca). **Mary Evans Picture Library:** Thaliastock (bl). **25 © The Trustees of the British Museum. All rights reserved:** (br). **Bridgeman Images:** Iberfoto (crb). **Dreamstime.com:** Dmitriy Moroz (ca). **27 Dreamstime.com:** Chris Hill (tr). **28 © The Trustees of the**

British Museum. All rights reserved: (clb). **Dreamstime.com:** Bernard Bialorucki (bc); Lefteris Papaulakis (cl). **29 Alamy Stock Photo:** imageBROKER (c). **© The Trustees of the British Museum. All rights reserved:** (clb). **30 © The Trustees of the British Museum. All rights reserved:** (clb). **Photo Scala, Florence:** RMN-Grand Palais / Dist. (cl). **31 Alamy Stock Photo:** Heritage Image Partnership Ltd (ca). **32 Getty Images:** CM Dixon / Print Collector (bc). **33 Bridgeman Images:** Luisa Ricciarini (c). **© The Trustees of the British Museum. All rights reserved:** (c). **Photo Scala, Florence:** Courtesy of the Ministero Beni e Att. Culturali e del Turismo (ca). **34 Dreamstime.com:** Boggy (c). **35 Alamy Stock Photo:** Nataliya Nazarova (ca). **Mary Evans Picture Library:** Antiquarian Images (cl). **36 Bridgeman Images:** (cl). **37 Alamy Stock Photo:** GRANGER – Historical Picture Archive (tr). **Dreamstime.com:** Kmiragaya (bc). **Shutterstock.com:** Murat Tegmen (crb). **38 Alamy Stock Photo:** Peter Horree (tc). **Dreamstime.com:** Sean Pavone (ca). **Mary Evans Picture Library:** (clb). **39 Alamy Stock Photo:** Alex Segre (tr). **40 Alamy Stock Photo:** Pictures Now (tr). **Getty Images:** Claude Gariepy (bc). **41 Bridgeman Images:** (cr); Alinari (cb). **42 Bridgeman Images:** Chester Beatty Library (br). **Dreamstime.com:** Friptuleac Roman (clb). **Getty Images:** Universal History Archive / Universal Images Group (c). **43 Getty Images:** Daniele Schneider / Photononstop (crb). **44 Getty Images / iStock:** Felix Friebe (tl). **45 Alamy Stock Photo:** David Grossman (clb); Heritage Image

Partnership Ltd (br). **46 Alamy Stock Photo:** Tibor Bognar (cl). **Dreamstime.com:** Radiokafka (cb); Dmitry Rukhlenko (crb). **Los Angeles County Museum of Art:** From the Nasli and Alice Heeramaneck Collection (bc). **47 Dreamstime.com:** Milosk50 (clb). **Los Angeles County Museum of Art:** Purchased with funds provided by Christian Humann (tr). **48 Alamy Stock Photo:** GRANGER – Historical Picture Archive (bc). **Dorling Kindersley:** The Science Museum, London (cr). **49 Getty Images:** Asian Art & Archaeology, Inc. / CORBIS (br). **Robert Harding Picture Library:** Tim Graham (cr). **50 Bridgeman Images:** Dirk Bakker (bc). **Mary Evans Picture Library:** Album (ca). **Dreamstime.com:** Tim Graham (cra). **51 Alamy Stock Photo:** Heritage Image Partnership Ltd (bc). **Bridgeman Images:** Photo © The Detroit Institute of Arts (ca). **Getty Images / iStock:** miralex (cr). **52 Alamy Stock Photo:** Design Pics (bc); Horizon International Images (br). **53 Bridgeman Images:** Werner Forman Archive (bc). **54 Alamy Stock Photo:** CPA Media Pte Ltd (cl). **Bridgeman Images:** Getty Images: zhangguifu (tr). **55 Alamy Stock Photo:** The Print Collector (tr). **Shutterstock.com:** Milos Vymazal (br). **57 Alamy Stock Photo:** janniwet wangkiri (bl). **Dreamstime.com:** Serge Bertasius (tr); Icon72 (bc). **58 Dreamstime.com:** Pablo Caridad (cra). **59 © The Trustees of the British Museum. All rights reserved:** (clb). **Dreamstime.com:** Boguslaw Chyla (br); Saiko3p (tl); Gbor Koves (cra). **61 Dreamstime.com:** Martyn Unsworth (bl).

All other images © Dorling Kindersley

Great pictorial atlases from DK

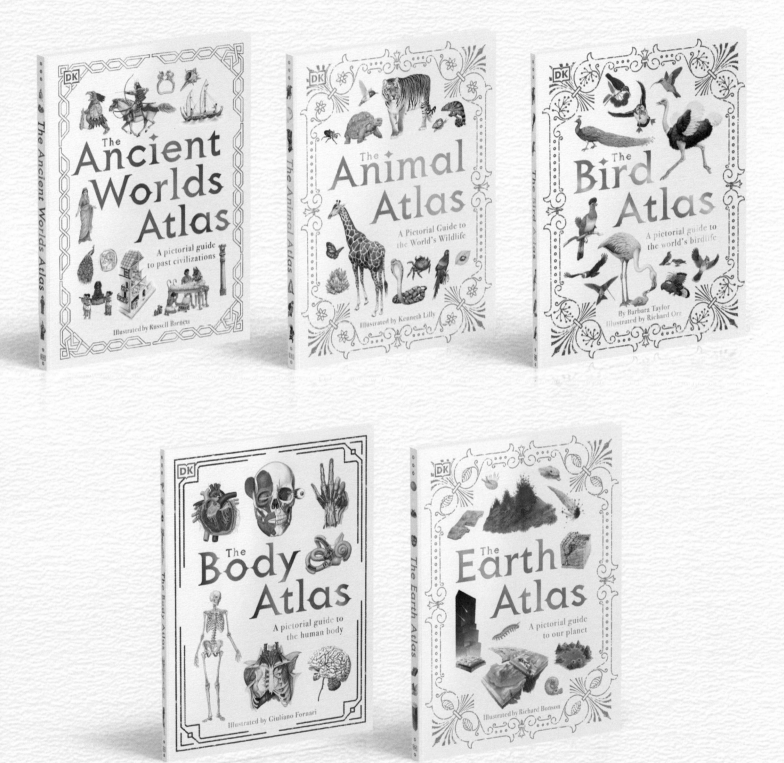